Northwestern University
STUDIES IN *Phenomenology* &
Existential Philosophy

GENERAL EDITOR
John Wild

ASSOCIATE EDITOR
James M. Edie

CONSULTING EDITORS
Herbert Spiegelberg
William Earle
George A. Schrader
Maurice Natanson
Paul Ricoeur
Aron Gurwitsch
Calvin O. Schrag
Hubert L. Dreyfus

Themes from
the Lectures

Maurice Merleau-Ponty

Translated by

Themes from the Lectures at the Collège de France 1952–1960

JOHN O'NEILL

NORTHWESTERN UNIVERSITY PRESS
EVANSTON   1 9 7 0

John O'Neill is Associate Professor of Sociology
at York University, Toronto, Ontario.
He is the author
of *Perception, Expression, and History: The Social
Phenomenology of Maurice Merleau-Ponty*
and the translator of *Humanism and Terror* by
Merleau-Ponty.

Contents

Translator's Preface

CLAUDE LEFORT HAS MADE IT impossible for anyone working on the texts left by Maurice Merleau-Ponty not to begin with some reflections upon Merleau-Ponty's "unfinished thought." [1] I can hardly hope to approach the profundity and eloquence of Lefort's meditations upon that interrogation which creates out of the philosopher's working life a human document that arouses in us those questions through which the world and history bring us to the mystery of being and expression. Yet, as Lefort himself has found, it seems natural to speak of Merleau-Ponty's work in the same style forged by its own persistent digging at the roots of perception, nature, and his-

1. Maurice Merleau-Ponty, *The Visible and the Invisible, Followed by Working Notes,* ed. Claude Lefort, trans. Alphonso Lingis (Evanston: Northwestern University Press, 1968).

tory.[2] Because his working method was to proceed indirectly toward the enigma of philosophical discourse itself, Merleau-Ponty's philosophical life of its own nature leaves us with the unfinished work of *The Visible and the Invisible,* as well as the *Introduction to the Prose of the World.*[3] Thus the silences within his life no less than his death belong essentially to his work and to his own temperament.

The themes from Merleau-Ponty's lectures at the Collège de France are an invaluable source for tracing the progression and complex interweaving of his theories of perception, language, and history. Gradually we can see Merleau-Ponty moving toward a radical ontology of truth, nature, and philosophical interrogation which was still unfinished in *The Visible and the Invisible.* We can also understand the profundity of the shorter essay on the visible, *L'Oeil et l'esprit,*[4] in which the ontological presuppositions of modern science are examined in a manner reminiscent of Husserl's argument in the *Krisis der europäischen Wissenschaften,*[5] but in the context of

2. John O'Neill, *Perception, Expression, and History: The Social Phenomenology of Merleau-Ponty* (Evanston: Northwestern University Press, 1970).

3. Maurice Merleau-Ponty, "Introduction to the Prose of the World," trans. John O'Neill, *Tri-Quarterly,* Spring 1970.

4. Maurice Merleau-Ponty, "Eye and Mind," trans. Carleton Dallery, in *The Primacy of Perception and Other Essays,* ed. James M. Edie (Evanston: Northwestern University Press, 1964).

5. Edmund Husserl, *The Crisis of European Sciences and Transcendental Phenomenology,* trans. David Carr (Evanston: Northwestern University Press, 1970).

Merleau-Ponty's own phenomenology of art and embodiment.

> Scientific thinking, a thinking which looks on from above, and thinks of the object-in-general, must return to the "there is" which underlies it; to the site, the soil of the sensible and opened world such as it is in our life and for our body—not that possible body which we may legitimately think of as an information machine but that actual body I call mine, this sentinel standing quietly at the command of my words and my acts. Further, *associated bodies* must be brought forward along with my body—the "others," not merely as my congeners, as the zoologist says, but the others who haunt me and whom I haunt; the "others" along *with* whom I haunt a single, present, and actual Being as no animal ever haunted those beings of his own species, locale or habitat. In this primordial historicity, science's agile and improvisatory thought will learn to ground itself upon things themselves and upon itself, and will once more become philosophy.[6]

The voice of Merleau-Ponty is not lost to us for the simple reason that, whether in lecturing or writing, Merleau-Ponty never used language as a mere tool or index of his thought. He rejected the logical stripping of language, not because he was heedless of clarity but because logic leads to the construction of a world from which man is absent and, with him, the consequences of time, that is, of magic, myth, and poetry. Merleau-Ponty's fascination with language and symbols, the wonder of art and vision, the

6. *The Primacy of Perception,* pp. 160–61.

ambivalence of history and action, is a fascination with the origin of things, nature, and man. Thus Merleau-Ponty's own language seems to caress the contours of things; often his thoughts achieve a tactile quality which results in a cathexis of thought and being, a logos, in which the word becomes flesh. In short, there is a magic in Merleau-Ponty's language which makes being sensible to us and in turn opens us to its peculiar solicitation. Whether he wrote of nature, art, language, or politics, Merleau-Ponty always struggled to unearth those moments or junctures in which meaning and experience reverse themselves without privilege upon one another.

> In a sense the whole of philosophy, as Husserl says, consists in restoring a power to signify, a birth of meaning, or a wild meaning, an expression of experience by experience, which in particular clarifies the special domain of language. And, in a sense, as Valéry said, language is everything, since it is the voice of the things, the waves and the forests. And what we have to understand is that there is no dialectical reversal from one of these views to the other; we do not have to reassemble them into a synthesis: they the special domain of language. And, in a sense, as truth.[7]

We can never accept the artificialism of science, even with respect to nature, and far less with respect to language, politics, or history. Language, history, science, and politics are all human activities, which can only be understood in terms of human commit-

7. *The Visible and the Invisible*, p. 155.

ments, or as situated activities grounded in the everyday world. We do not invent our language any more than we invent our history. Rather, we find ourselves in history just as we do in our language. We owe to language the assurance of the exchange of thoughts and values and thereby our notions of a common mankind and a universal history. The foundations of the human sciences do not rest upon any object, properly speaking, or on any theoretical construction, but in the institution between ourselves and others of meanings and values which each of us undertakes according to his situation and yet by which we are drawn into the drama of a universal culture. Historical knowledge joins in the archaeological explorations of phenomenology, not in search of any philosophical foundation but for a radical point of departure from which consciousness institutes the recovery of itself and its world.

> Thus what we understand by the concept of *institution* are those events in experience which endow it with durable dimensions, in relation to which a whole series of other experiences will require meaning, will form an intelligible series or a history—or again those events which sediment in me a meaning, not just as survivals or residues, but as the invitation to a sequel, the necessity of a future.[8]

Merleau-Ponty understood the whole of human culture as a search into the past, a quest reaching to the future in which each of us engages whether

8. See below, pp. 40–41.

in speaking, writing, thinking, building, or dreaming. In this fashion, the past and what we can make of it lives in us; it is not something we can survey apart from ourselves, and if it speaks to us it is because we are able to involve it in our own problems and needs. Human culture is necessarily instrumental or artificial because it is the product of language and our relations with others, which it in turn supports ideally.

> Ideality coincides with historicity because it rests upon acts and because "the only way to grasp an idea is to produce it." The idea is impalpable and invisible because it has been *made*. The historicity of an idea is not the fact of its conclusion in a series of events with a unique temporal location, or its origin in the mind of a particular man living at a certain place and time. It is its function to situate a task which is not uniquely its own, but one that echoes back to earlier beginnings. The historicity of an idea summons up the whole past and the entire future of culture as its witness. And to call upon so much history it has no need of documents, for history has its anchorage within itself, in the flesh of its sensible or natural existence, its active and productive being. It has only to reflect in order to know that thought makes itself, that it is culture and history.[9]

It is in speech, above all, that I am aware of myself as an activity which between me and others recovers the passive and silent being which I am in the telling toward what I have in mind to say. In speech we articulate self, objects and others in a structure

9. See below, pp. 116–17.

which is *presence* borne along vectors of intentionality which trace the style of the world around us as irremediably our own, as "la cariatide de nos efforts qui convergent du seul fait qu'ils sont efforts d'expression." Thus language is neither the pale shadow of thought nor the simple mnemonic of practice. Language is the orientation of the speaking subject in his everyday world where the search for meaning, like the question "Where am I?" belongs to our ways of situating ourselves among things, and is rather a simple appeal for the elucidation of the things we know and not at all a question about the idea of knowing.

JOHN O'NEILL

Themes from
the Lectures

1 / The Sensible World
and the
World of Expression

CONTEMPORARY THINKERS READILY ADMIT that the sensible world and sensible consciousness should be described in terms of what is original to them. But everything continues as though such descriptions did not affect our definition of being and subjectivity. Whenever the higher forms of consciousness and judgment are studied, it is almost always in terms of the thinking subject defined as the pure power of bestowing significations and the capacity of absolute survey. Any attempt to take account of the finitude of sensible consciousness is rejected as a return to naturalism or even pantheism. In contrast, we propose to show that the philosopher learns from his contact with perception an awareness of a relation to being which necessitates and makes possible a new analysis of the understanding. For the meaning of a perceived object when picked out from all others still does not stand isolated from the constellation in which it appears; it is articulated only as a certain *distance* in relation to the order of space, time, motion, and signification in general in which we are established. The meaning of an object is given only as a systematic deformation of our universe of experience, without our ever being able to name its operative principle. Every perception is the perception of something solely by way of being at the same time the relative imperception of a horizon or background which it implies but does not thematize. Perceptual consciousness is therefore indirect or even inverted in relation to an ideal of adequation which it presumes but never encounters directly. Thus if we understand the perceived world as an open field, it would be just as absurd to reduce everything else to this as to impose upon it a "universe of ideas" which owed nothing to it. There is truly a reversal when one passes from the sensible world, in which we are caught, to a world of expression, where we seek to capture significations to serve our purpose, although this reversal and the "retrogressive movement" of truth are solicited by a perceptual anticipation. Properly speaking, the expression which language makes possible resumes and amplifies another expression which is revealed in the "archaeology" of the perceived world.

We have studied the phenomenon of movement as an example of this transition and reversal. There we showed that the simplest perception of movement presupposes a subject who is situated spatially and initiated into the world, and that, from its own side, movement becomes charged with all the meaning scattered in the sensible world and in the silent arts becomes a universal means of expression.

The description of motion as a change in location or variation in the relations between a "mobile" and its coordinates is a retrospective schema, an ulterior formulation of our bodily experience of movement. Once motion is cut off from its perceptual origins, it defies representation and is self-destructive, as has often been shown since Zeno. But to give an intelligible account of motion it is enough to go back, as suggested by Bergson, to the internal experience of motion, in other words, to our *own* movement. We have to understand how the immediate unity of our gesture is able to spread itself over external experiences and introduce into them the possibility of a transition which from the standpoint of objective thought is unreal. We consider the research in Gestalt theory to be valuable for the manner in which it delimits this problem. Thus when two fixed points are projected in succession on a screen they are seen as two traces of a single movement in which they even lose their distinct existence. Here what happens is that the external forces insert themselves into a system of equivalents that is ready to function and in which they operate upon us, like signs in a language, not by arousing their uniquely correspondent significations but, like mileposts, in a process which is still unfolding, or as though they were picking out a path which, as it

were, inspired them from a distance. Thus perception is already expression. But this natural language
does not isolate; it does not "bring out" what is
expressed, but allows it to adhere in its own way
more to the "perceptual chain" than to the "verbal
chain." When Gestalt theorists show that the perception of motion depends upon numerous *figural
moments* and ultimately on the whole structure of
the field, they are sketching in the same way as the
perceiving subject a sort of *thinking apparatus*
which is his incarnate and habitual being. The ac-
complishment of motion and change of location em-
anate from a field structure apart from which they
are unintelligible. Michotte's studies have shown all
the transitions between these configurations and the
perception of movement; for example, how the
movements of "natation" and "reptation" arise from
the very articulation and internal logic of the pho-
nemes. The same order of images, depending upon
the cadence in which they follow, can give an observer the impression of a petrified mineral world,
or of organic or animal life (Epstein). The quality
of the sound from a wind instrument bears the
mark and the organic rhythm of the breath from
which it came, as can be shown by the strange
impression received by reversing the normal register
of the sounds. Far from being a simple "displacement," movement is inscribed in the texture of the
shapes or qualities and is, so to speak, the revelation
of their being. There is, as someone has said, a

space and motion of which "the heart is sensible";
their prescription issues from the internal dynamics
of the spectacle and reaches a culmination of envelopment in spatial change. The synthesis of perception occurs "on the object" (J. Paliard) [1] and ultimately in the presence of the whole world; it is in
and by means of "implication" that the natural light
of perception opens its path.

One can only do justice to this allusive relation
to being if one undertakes an analysis of the subject
who is its source and retraces the birth in him of
what is properly called expression. In this task we
are aided by contemporary research on the body
schema. In these studies the body is the seat of a
certain praxis, the point from which there is something to do in the world, the register in which we are
inscribed and whose inscription we continue. Such
studies renew our conception of space and motion.
At every moment the body, as Head has remarked,
is a global awareness of distance already covered as
well as the means of installing us in advance in the
position toward which we are moving (Kohn-
stamm's phenomenon shows that our arm adopts
the position toward which it is moved by muscular
forces as though it were already acquired or "normal"). These constant or provisional norms reveal a
practical intimacy with space whose relationship to

1. Cf. *Phenomenology of Perception,* trans. Colin Smith
(London: Routledge and Kegan Paul; New York: Human-
ities Press, 1962), pp. 255n, 257n.—*Trans.*

spatial knowledge or gnosis is complex. On the one hand, gnosis is founded upon praxis, since the elementary notions of point, surface, and contour in the last analysis only have meaning for a subject modified by locality and himself situated in the space in which he unfolds the spectacle of a point of view. There is a kind of knowledge that is very close to praxis and can be damaged with it, as is shown in the failure to recognize certain geometric forms in certain apraxia (constructive apraxia). On the other hand, gnosic space is relatively independent of the practical expression of space, as is evident from pathological cases where serious practical impairments are compatible with ability to handle spatial symbols. The relative autonomy of superstructures which outlast the practical conditions which generated them—or can at least for a time hide their collapse—permits us to say with equal truth that we are conscious because we are mobile or that we are mobile because we are conscious. Consciousness, in the sense of knowledge, and movement, in the sense of displacement in objective space, are two abstract moments of a living structure which can very well extend its limits but would also destroy its powers if it were to abolish those limits. Insofar as psychology and psychopathology locate praxis and recognize it as an original domain they are in position to understand the strict relations between mobility and all the symbolic functions as well as to renew our conception of understanding. The analysis of Gerstmann's [2] syndrome (finger agnosia, failure to distinguish left from right, constructive and calculative apraxia) shows the hand to be a "theater where the visual, the linguistic, the spatial, the practical and the constructive seem to converge" (Lange). The body is the vehicle of an indefinite number of symbolic systems whose intrinsic development definitely surpasses the signification in "natural" gestures, but would collapse if ever the body ceases to prompt their operation and install them in the world and our life. Sleep dedifferentiates our praxical functions, beginning with the most subtle, the phonetic system, down to the most elementary, to the point where deep sleep without dreams has been compared to a state of apraxia. Inversely, upon waking the clarity of consciousness restores our diacritical and antithetical systems through which our slumbering relation to the world is quickly disarticulated and annulled. These correlations are examples of the mutation or sublimation which in man transform mobility into symbolic gesticulation and implicit expression into open expression.

As a counter theory, in the last part of the course we outlined the study of movement as a means of universal expression. This theme will be taken up again later (when we will also go into the analysis of linguistic gesticulation which we have

2. J. Gerstmann, "Reine Taktile Agnosie," *Monatsschrift für Psychiatrie und Neurologie*, XLIV (1918), 329–42.—*Trans.*

left aside altogether for another year). We restricted ourselves to examples drawn from the use of movement in painting and cinematic art. Painting does not copy movement point by point or by offering us signs of it; it invents *emblems* which give it a substantial presence, presenting it to us as the "metamorphosis" (Rodin) of one attitude into another, the implication of a future within the present. Now if even change of location can be pictured in this way and be conveyed and understood by symbols which do not move, we can understand how in the history of painting the category of movement develops far beyond simple local displacement. We can see, for example, how pictorial representation, in contrast to lineal representation, can be considered a development of movement in painting. Finally, we speak of movement in painting every time the world is presented indirectly by means of open forms, oblique or partial aspects. From the simplest perception of movement to the experience of painting, we are always faced with the same paradox of a force legible in a form, a trace or signature of time in space. The cinema, invented as a means of photographing objects in movement or as a *representation of movement,* has discovered in the process much more than change in location, namely a new way of symbolizing thoughts, *the movement of representation.* For in the film, in the cutting, editing and changes of perspective, there is a solicitation and, so to speak, a celebration of our openness to the world and to the other person, an openness upon which the film can make continuous variations. The film no longer plays with objective movements, as it did at first, but with changes of perspective which define the shift from one person to another or his merging with the action. In this respect especially, film is still as far as ever from offering us all that we might have expected of it.

Through the study of linguistic symbolism, by taking account of the world of speech as well as the world of expression, we shall be in a position to ascertain definitively the philosophical meaning of the preceding analyses, of the problem of the relation between "natural" expression and cultural expression. We shall then be able to decide whether the dialectic of nature is immanent in our spirit, or whether we should seek a third philosophy beyond this dilemma.

2 / Studies in the Literary Use of Language

FOR THE MOST PART the theory of language confines itself to so-called exact forms, that is to say, to observations about thoughts that have already matured in the person speaking and are at least immanent in the person listening. The result is that such theory loses sight of the heuristic value of language, how it works to gain mastery—which, on the contrary, is clearly seen in the writer at work. Perhaps constituted language should be regarded a secondary form derived from the initial operation which establishes a new signification in a linguistic apparatus constructed with old signs and thus able only to indicate the new meaning or draw the reader and the author himself toward it.

For its own part, literature has been in advance of the interest shown in it by the philosophy of language. For a century now writers have always been more aware of what is singular and even problematic in their calling. Writing is no longer (if it ever was) the simple enunciation of what one has conceived. It is working with a tool which at times produces more and at times less than one has put into it, and this is simply the result of a series of paradoxes that make the writer's craft an exhausting and never-ending task. The paradox of the true and the imaginary, truer than truth—of intentions and achievement, often unexpected and always *other*—of speech and silence, in which expression can fail from being overly deliberate and succeed to the extent that it remains indirect—of the subjective and the objective, in which a writer's deepest secret, still barely articulated inside him, surrenders itself in all clarity to a public which his work creates for itself, while what he possesses most consciously remains by contrast a dead letter—finally, the paradox of the author and the man, where it is evident that it is the man's lived experience which provides the substance of his work and yet, in order *to become true*, needs an elaboration that is the very thing which cuts the writer off from the living community; in other words, all these surprises and traps force literature to see itself as a problem and drive the writer to ask "What is Literature?" [1] thus raising questions not only about his practice but even more about his theory of language. It is this type of question that we have tried to put to the work of Valéry and Stendhal.

1. Jean-Paul Sartre, *What is Literature?* trans. Bernard Frechtman (New York: Harper & Row, 1965).

The use to which Valéry puts language can only be understood if we take into account the long period in which he had killed himself—or wrote only for himself. From the notebooks of 1900 to 1910 (which later formed the two collections *Tel Quel I* and *II*) one can see that his mistrust of language was not just a special case of his distrust of a life which supported itself only by unintelligible prodigies. It is incomprehensible that the body should be both an inert mass which marks our place during sleep and the lively instrument which, for example, in the service of a painter does what it wants to do better than consciousness. It is incomprehensible that the spirit should be a power of doubt, interrogation, reservation, and disengagement which makes us "inalienable" and "unattachable," and at the same time should merge and surrender itself to everything that happens, and that it is precisely by its "indefinite refusal to be anything whatsoever" that it actually constructs and becomes something. It is incomprehensible that I, who am irreducibly alien to all my roles, feel myself moved by my appearance in the gaze of others and that I in turn reflect an image of them that can affect them, so that there is woven between us an "exchange," a "chiasm between two 'destinies' . . ." in which there are never quite two of us and yet one is never alone. These absurdities are most pronounced in language and literature. Language is clear provided one passes over the words quickly enough, but this "fundamental solidity" collapses before a rigorous consciousness. Literature also lives through an imposture: the writer says what his language wants and passes for profound; each lack in him, once it is put into words, becomes a powerful form, and the sum of the accidents which go to make a book appears as the author's intention. At the outset, Valéry could only write "out of weakness" or from cynicism, putting into words all the reasons he had for distrusting words and constructing a work on the negation of all work.

Nevertheless, in the exercise of literature this nihilism is overcome in fact and in principle. However impossible language may have been, it was there. Moreover, there was at least one form of language which one could not reject precisely because it did not pretend *to say something*—namely, poetry. Now, upon examination it became clear that the reason why poetry does not convey signification by effacing itself before what it says, like a plain statement, and is not detached from its words is not simply because poetry is like a song or dance of language, nor is it for want of signification, but it is because it always has more than one signification. Thus it was necessary to admit, at least in the case of poetry, the "miracle" of a "mystical union" of sound and meaning, despite everything we know of the historical accidents that go to make up each language. But once this prodigy has been discovered in poetry in the strict sense, it can be found again in "that endlessly active poetry which torments static language, opening or narrowing the meaning of words, through symmetry or conversions, and which at every moment alters the fiduciary value of this currency." These variations in language, which at first appear to support the skeptic, are ultimately the proof of its meaning, since words would not change in meaning unless they were trying to say something. Thus, relative to a certain state of language—and even if it has to be renewed from one age to another—the attempt to achieve expression has been a success or a failure, either saying something or saying nothing. The justification of poetry rehabilitates the whole of language, and in the end Valéry admits that even the intellectual is not a pure consciousness, illuminated all the more by the refusal to identify with anything whatsoever, and that our clarity comes from our commerce with the world and with others, as we gradually constitute ourselves a system of capacities, which he calls "implex" or "animal of words," that is that hybrid or bastard that guarantees below the level of the will the connection between what we are doing and what we wanted to do. From the contempt of literature as a literary theme there is a transition to a consciously accepted literature, a shift from a definite refusal of any identification whatsoever to the desire to speak and write. "Shall I be on top of my art? I am alive" (*Mon Faust*). Men are "hybrids" of body and spirit, but what is called spirit is inseparable from what is most precarious about them; for light would not illuminate a thing unless there were something to screen it. Precisely because it is radical, the critique of language and life completely merges with the practice of life and language. Valéry's last writings are truly the reply to the crisis of 1892 which led him to the rule of silence; their language sustains its own aim, its own ethic, and its own justification.

Stendhal's is also the story of an apprenticeship to speech. His vital problem, as it appears from the *Journal* for the years 1804 and 1805, lay in his inability, as he puts it, "to feel" and "to perceive" at the same time: on the one hand, he acts self-consciously but cynically and as if role-playing, and he is rightly told that he has not "penetrated" what he said; on the other hand, he surrenders to happiness, but then it is a "reverie" or an ecstasy which deprives him of the strength to go on and leaves him dumb. His first literary essays reveal the same self-misunderstanding; he begins to write for success and to achieve that ambition he relies upon observation almost to the point of a science of life. But unwittingly, and even while he was adopting the Code Civil as his model, he was making an apprenticeship to the inner dialogue in his *Journal.* Once he had given up the promotion of his literary and amatory projects and had opened himself and his writing to the revery he had at first resisted, he suddenly found himself capable of improvisation, conviction, creation. He realized that there is no conflict between truth and fiction, solitude and love, living and writing; and out of the first person, the *ego* which so easily lends itself to slipping into any role, he creates the means of an entirely new art. Henceforth he can consent to himself because in the practice of living and the practice of style he has gained the capacity to escape his separation.

The question remains whether this solution is just a writer's solution which only goes to the improvement of his work, whereas the speaking subject who is open to everything that can be said is, by this very fact, removed from the involvement of life. One could easily believe this on seeing, for example, what little stability Stendhal showed in face of political opinion. Nevertheless, through all the wavering from cynicism to candor, Stendhal did follow a line: he never wavered in his absolute refusal to accept ignorance and misery or in his belief that a man is not formed until he has "settled with reality," until he has escaped from the polite behavior through which his class rules him. Such denials are tantamount to the commitment to a cause. Stendhal is saying roughly that to be human is a political position. Perhaps the function of criticism is the writer's commitment. If it is true, as Stendhal believed, that all power is false, then perhaps we should not overlook the fact that all writers who are unprejudiced and open to the future know what they do not want better than what they do want. Perhaps all men, as well as the man of letters, can only be present to the world and others through language; and perhaps in everyone language is the basic function which constructs a life and its work and transforms even the problems of our existence into life's motives.

3 / The Problem of Speech

SPEECH DOES NOT SIMPLY ACTIVATE the possibilities inscribed in language. Already in Saussure,[1] in spite of his restrictive definitions, speech is far from being a simple effect; it modifies and sustains language just as much as it is conveyed through it. In reality, by adopting speech as his theme, Saussure broke new ground in the study of language and began for us a categorical revision. He challenged the rigid distinction between sign and signification which seemed evident when one considered instituted language alone, but breaks down in speech where sound and meaning are not simply associated. The well-known definition of the sign as "diacritical, oppositive, and negative" means that

1. F. de Saussure, *Cours de linguistique générale* (Paris: Payot, 1964); *Course in General Linguistics,* ed. Charles Bally and Albert Sechehaye with Albert Reidlinger, trans. Wade Baskin (New York: Philosophical Library, 1959).— *Trans.*

language is present in the speaking subject as a system of intervals between signs and significations, and that, as a unity, the act of speech simultaneously operates the differentiation of these two orders. Finally, it implies that the distinction between *res extensa* and *res cogitans* cannot be applied to significations that are not closed nor to signs that exist only in their interrelation.

The purpose of the course is to illustrate and to extend the Saussurian conception of speech as a positive and dominating function.

We have first applied it to the problem of the child's acquisition of language. A Saussurian like Roman Jakobson readily distinguishes between the mere factual presence of a sound or phoneme in the child's babbling and the proper linguistic possession of the same element as a means of signifying. The sudden tumble of sounds at the moment the child begins to speak comes about because, in order to be at his disposal as means of signification, the child must integrate the sounds into the system of phonetic contrasts upon which the language surrounding him is constructed and in some sense acquire the principles of that system. But Jakobson interprets this phenomenon in terms of a debatable psychology. Where the problem is to understand how the child appropriates the phonetic system and at the same time is suddenly in possession of the melody of meaningful language that had previously "waited for meaning," Jakobson appeals to *attention* and *judgment*. In other words, Jakobson resorts to the functions of analysis and judgment, which in reality are dependent upon language and, moreover, inadequately account for the atypical aspect of signs and significations as being due to indiscrimination upon the child's part.

Recently, an advance was made in linking the acquisition of language to the whole series of developments through which the child assumes his surroundings and in particular his relations with others. However, this recourse to the affective context does not *explain* the acquisition of language. In the first place, the developments in the affective decentering are just as enigmatic as the context itself. Secondly, because, above all, language is not just the counterpart or replica of the affective context, it plays a role in it, introducing other motives, changing its internal meaning, and ultimately is itself a form of existence or a diversion within existence. Even subjects who fail to find an effective equilibrium learn to handle the tense of the verb which is supposedly correlated with the various dimensions of their life. The relations with others, intelligence, and language cannot be set out in a lineal and causal series: they belong to those cross-currents where *someone lives*. Speech, said Michelet, is our mother speaking. Thus while speech puts the child in a more profound relation to she who names everything and puts being into words, it also translates this relation into a more general order. The mother opens the child to circuits which from the very beginning flow out from the maternal surrounding which he will never again find through them. The enigma of man and speech is not reduced by "explanations in terms of affectivity." The latter serve only as occasions for the observation of what Freud called the "overdetermination" of speech, transcending "physical language," and for the description of aonther level of interaction between the concrete and the universal, perspective and horizon. The case of Helen Keller shows what an expansion and mediation speech can bring to the child's anger and anxiety, as well as how it can be a mask, a fictionalization as much as a genuine expression, as perhaps in those individuals who do not possess it fully. At all events, these various modalities of speech, which are just so many ways of relating us to the universal, bind speech to a *modus vivendi.*

We have sought further confirmation of the fundamental role of speech in certain pathological disintegrations, drawing upon Kurt Goldstein's work, *Language and Language Disturbances.*[2] In earlier works Goldstein distinguished between an automatic language (an "external verbal knowledge") and language in the full sense (genuine denomination), which is related to a "categorical attitude." The question arises whether these early distinctions put signification into language *like a pilot in a boat.* In the 1948 work, however, these two orders are related so that there is no longer signification on the one hand and the "instrumentalities" of language on

2. New York: Grune and Stratton, 1948.

the other. In the long run, the instrumentalities of language only remain functional as long as the categorical attitude is intact and, inversely, the impairment of the instrumentalities compromises the grasp of signification. There is thus a sort of spirit of language, a spirit always freighted with language. For language is the system of differentiations through which the individual articulates his relation to the world. The conception of neurological pathology in terms of dedifferentiation and the Saussurian notion of the diacritical sign are interrelated and akin to Humboldt's idea of language as a "perspective on the world." There is also a reminiscence of Humboldt in Goldstein's analysis of the "internal form of language" (*innere Sprachform*), which, according to him, mobilizes the instrumentalities of language, either in the perception of the verbal chain or in elocution. The spirit becomes dependent upon the linguistic organism which it has created, into which it continues to breathe life, though the latter in turn communicates its own impulse as though it had its own source of life. The categorical attitude is not an act of pure spirit, but presupposes a live functioning of the "internal forms of language." Instead of being framed in Kantian terms, the categorical attitude is now anchored in articulated language. For articulated language is able to manipulate empty symbols; it not only brings a surplus of meaning to a given situation, as in a cry or gesture, but can itself evoke its own context and induce the mental framework which is its source; in other words, it is, in the full sense of the word, expression. "We may say that the development of the categorical attitude is a function of the degree of development of language toward eminently conventional forms in which, as we have said, the maximum of indeterminacy in the symbols yields the maximum determination of the object." [3] Although none of the authors mentions him, one can recognize in this immanent spirit of language the mediator which Saussure called speech.

Again, it is this same spirit of language that the writer encounters professionally. The act of writing, says Proust, is in a sense the opposite of speech and life because it opens us to others as they are at the same time that it closes us to ourselves. The writer's speech, on the contrary, itself creates an "allocutor" capable of understanding and imposes a private world upon him as something evident. But in doing so it only reactivates the original operation of language with the deliberate aim of acquiring and putting into circulation not just the statistical and common aspects of the world, but its very manner of touching and inserting itself into the individual's experience. It cannot therefore be content with the established and current significations. Just as the painter and the musician make use of objects, colors, and sounds in order to reveal the relations between the elements of the world in a living unity—

3. A. Ombredane, *L'Aphasie et l'élaboration de la pensée explicite* (Paris: Presses Universitaires de France, 1951), pp. 370–71.

for example, the metaphorical correspondences in a marine landscape—so the writer takes everyday language and makes it deliver the prelogical participation of landscapes, dwellings, localities, and gestures, of men among themselves and with us. In literature, ideas, as in music and painting, are not the "ideas of the intellect"; they are never quite detached from what the author sees; they are transparent, as unchallengeable as persons, but not definable. What has been called Proust's Platonism is an attempt at an integral expression of the perceived or lived world. For this reason, the writer's work is a work of language rather than of "thought." His task is to produce a system of signs whose internal articulation reproduces the contours of experience; the reliefs and sweeping lines of these contours in turn generate a syntax in depth, a mode of composition and recital which breaks the mold of the world and everyday language and refashions it. This new speech takes shape in the writer unnoticed, during years of apparently idle living in which he despairs of the lack of literary ideas and "subjects"—until one day he yields to the weight of that *way of speaking* which has gradually been built up in him and he starts to say how he became a writer, creating a work from the story of the birth of that work. Thus literary speech expresses the world insofar as it has been given to someone to live it and at the same time it absorbs the world and poses itself as its proper goal. Proust was right, therefore, when he stressed that speech or writing could become a manner of living. He would have been wrong to think (which he did not) that this way of life more than any other could embrace and suffer everything. However, no one has better expressed the vicious circle or prodigy of speech, that to speak or to write is truly to *translate* an experience which, without the word that it inspires, would not become a text. "The book of unknown signs within me (signs in relief it seemed, for my attention, as it explored my unconscious in its search, struck against them, circled round them like a diver sounding) no one could help me read by any rule, for its reading consists in an act of creation in which no one can take our place and in which no one can collaborate." [4]

These descriptions of the inchoate, regressive, and sublimated forms of speech should enable us to study its relation in principle to instituted language and to clarify the nature of institution as the act of the birth of all possible speech. This will form the topic of another course. [5]

4. Marcel Proust, *A la recherche du temps perdu*, II, 23.
5. Probably a reference to the course on "Institution in Personal and Public History," chapter 5 below.

4 / Materials for a Theory of History

THE CONCEPT OF HISTORY must be disentangled from a number of confusions. It is often argued as though there were, on the one hand, a philosophy which ascribes to man values ascertainable outside of time, a consciousness unrestricted by any interest in actual events, and, on the other hand, those "philosophies of history" which discover in the flow of events an occult logic whose outcome we can only wait upon. We should then have to choose between the wisdom of an understanding which does not flatter itself upon discovering a meaning to history, but merely tries constantly to bend history toward our values, and a fanaticism that in the name of the secret of history gleefully overturns the most evident of our beliefs. But this is an artificial cleavage: there is no question of choosing between external events and the internal spirit of man, between history and the timeless. All the instances that one might care to oppose to history have their own history through which they communicate with history, although they have their own way of using time. Furthermore, nothing, not even a political movement, is enclosed in a moment of time and in this sense it is not *in* history, for the most passionate stances can have an inexhaustible bearing—like a monogram of the spirit in things.

The real problem is always hidden by traditional discussions of historical materialism. It does not matter so much to know that one is a "spiritualist" or a "materialist" in his approach to history as to know how one understands the spirit and the material of history. There are conceptions of the "spiritual" which so isolate it from human life that it is as inert as matter, and there can be a "historical materialism" which incorporates the whole of man in the economic and social struggle. History effects an exchange between all levels of activity so that none of them can be dignified with exclusive causality. The question is rather to know if this concatenation of the problems is an indication of the simultaneity of their resolution or whether this convergence and recuperation exists only in the process of interrogation.

The proper starting point is not from the alternatives of understanding and history or spirit and matter, but from those of history as an unknown god—the good or evil genius—and history as the milieu of life. History is a milieu of life if it can be said that there is, between theory and practice, between culture and man's labor, between epochs and individual lives, between planned actions and the time in which they mature, an affinity that is neither fortuitous nor grounded in an omnipotent logic. Historical action is invented and yet it responds so well to the problems of the time that it is understood and followed, so that, as Péguy said, it incorporates itself into the "public duration." It would be simply a retrospective illusion to project the historical act into the past which it transforms. But, similarly, it would be a *prospective illusion* to bring the present to a halt on the threshold of an empty future, as though each present did not prolong itself toward a horizon of the future, and as though the meaning of a period which is decided by human initiative were *nothing* before that. Historical invention works through a matrix of open and unfinished significations presented by the present. Like the touch of a sleepwalker, it touches in things only what they have in them that belongs to the future. If the historical talent of great men were only a technique for manipulating others, there would surely be those adventures in history which endure and are always part of its scenery, but history would lack those exemplary actions which constitute a step into the public duration and inscribe themselves in the human memory, whether they last a month, a year, or a century. There is no history where the course of events is a series of episodes without unity, or where it is a struggle already decided in the heaven of ideas. History is there where there is a logic *within* contingence, a reason *within* unreason, where there is a historical perception which, like perception in general, leaves in the background what cannot enter the foreground but seizes the lines of force as they are generated and actively leads their traces to a conclusion. This analogy should not be interpreted as a shameful organicism or finalism, but as a reference to the fact that all symbolic systems—perception, language, history—only become what they were although in order to do so they need to be taken up into human initiative.

This idea of history was not systematically developed in this course. We tried to outline it through the researches of such people as Max Weber and his pupil Georg Lukács (particularly in *Geschichte und Klassenbewusstsein*, Berlin, 1923), who confirm the necessity of a path between the philosophy of understanding and the dogmatic philosophies of history.

As a point of departure, Max Weber gives particular attention to the radical contingency and infinity of the historical fact. From a "Kantian" perspective, historical objectivity therefore appears simply as the correlative of the historian's theoretical operation. It cannot flatter itself with having exhausted the reality of *history which has passed*. For, being in principle always tentative, it can only illuminate one aspect of an event and is lacking in any methodical abstraction which would eliminate other aspects of the event; thus of itself it calls forth further analyses and points of view. Max Weber is led by this antithesis between reality and constructed objectivity to draw an absolute contrast between the attitude of knowledge, which is always provisional and conditional, and practice, where on the contrary we encounter reality and assume the infinite task of evaluating the event as it happens, taking a position without any possibility of reprieve and under condi-tions quite contrary to those presupposed by theoret-ical justification. In practice we inevitably find our-selves in conflict and our decisions both justifiable and unjustifiable. Weber leaves the two spheres of knowledge and practice juxtaposed without any re-lation, and within the latter the conflicting options of the ethic of responsibility and the ethic of faith. This attitude is a constant feature of his career. It makes out of history a sort of malefactor.

However, in his empirical studies Weber disre-gards these antitheses. He starts with the observa-tion that there is a profound analogy between the task of the historian who undertakes to understand events and that of the man of action when prepar-ing his decision. Knowledge is gained by putting ourselves in the position of those who have acted; it is action in the realm of the imagination. But action is an anticipation of knowledge; it makes us histori-ans of our own lives. With regard to the radical pluralism of options, even a "polytheistic" system establishes a hierarchy among its gods. Moreover, a persistent profession of polytheism would imply *a certain* image of historical reality. The conflicting options of the ethic of responsibility and the ethic of faith are not exclusive. For even pure faith chooses the moment to declare its sincerity and the calculation of consequences is often a veiled judgment of value. Weber concludes with the admission (*Politik als Beruf*) [1] that here we are dealing with abstract limits between which, for better or worse, we try to steer in our daily politics.

This presupposes or entails a re-examination of the concept of history. It must be that *what has happened* should not be a reality in principle inimical to knowledge. Whatever comes to pass, however unfathomable it may be, must not conceal any "positive irrationality." And so, indeed, in such analyses as his famous study of *The Protestant Ethic and the Spirit of Capitalism*, Weber penetrates the interior of the historical fact far beyond what his "Kantian" principles allowed him and goes beyond the theoretical construction in the direction of historical "comprehension." He undertakes to get at the fundamental "choice" in the Calvinist ethic and the "affinity" of that choice with those other choices in Western history which, in conjunction with it, made capitalist enterprise possible (namely, the establishment of science and technology, law, and the state). The notion of an "affinity of choices" (*Wahlverwandtschaft*) makes the event something other than a conjunction of circumstances but without it appearing as an imminent historical necessity. It is

---

1. Max Weber, "Politics as a Vocation," in *From Max Weber: Essays in Sociology*, trans. and ed. H. H. Gerth and C. Wright Mills (New York: Oxford University Press, 1958). —*Trans.*

as though it were only in contact with one another that these choices together were able finally to produce Western capitalism, without the essence of the system pre-existing their encounter. Pluralism, which formerly seemed to ban any attempt at a unified interpretation of history, on the contrary now attests the solidarity of the economic order, and those of politics, law, morals, or religion as soon as the economic order itself is treated as the choice of a relation between men and with the world and takes its place in the logic of choice. Even the metamorphosis of the past by the conception which succeeds it presupposes a sort of understanding in depth between the present and the past. Our views would not overturn the image of the past if they were not "interested" in it, if they didn't envisage the totality of man, if our age were content with itself, or unless the past and the present belonged to a single realm of culture, that is to say, the replies that man freely makes to a permanent questioning. Our contact with our age is an initiation into every age; man is a historian because he belongs to history and history is only the amplification of practice.

History is no longer a tête-à-tête between a Kantian understanding and a past in itself; understanding now discovers in its object its own origins. The methodical attitude of the "objective" historian itself becomes part of a more inclusive history and is a species of that "rationalization" which at other levels produces capitalist society and the state, in the modern sense. Thus there is in Weber the outlines

of a phenomenology of historical choices which uncovers the intelligible matrices into which the infinite detail of facts is inserted. This phenomenology
is quite different from Hegel's because the meaning
which it discovers in historical facts is unstable and
always threatened. Capitalism denatures the Calvinist ethic from which it arises and preserves only its
external form or "shell," as Weber says. Historical
experience is never absolutely conclusive because
the question which moves it transforms itself along
the way. As a reply to a question poorly posed,
historical experience is itself equivocal. The "rationalization," the demystification of the world, comprises both gains and losses, for it is also a "disen-
chantment" and makes the order of the day, in
Weber's phrase, a "petrified" humanity. And so the
logic of choices is not necessarily extrapolated into a
confirmable future in which the problem *treated* by
Calvinism and capitalism would finally be *resolved*.
The philosophy of history does not add the revela-
tions of a universal history to the certitudes of the
understanding. It is rather through an unending
interrogation that all the ages together compose a
single and universal history.

The interest of what has come to be an old book
of Lukács' is that it attempts to push the comprehension of history further than Weber and thus to
rejoin Marxian intuitions—providing an opportunity to examine the possibility of a historical dialectic free from any dogmatic tutelage, having become a genuine *concrete dialectic*.

Lukács takes the present as his point of departure in aiming at a view of the totality which is
intended to appear only as a "totality of experience."
Lukács resumes the Weberian intuition of capitalism as "rationalization," and he determines its species and animation by developing its pre-capitalist
past and the post-capitalist future and by compre-
hending it as a process and not an immobile essence.
In comparison with pre-capitalist civilizations, capitalism represents the very embodiment of society
(*Vergesellschaftung der Gesellschaft*). In so-called
primitive civilizations collective life is in part imaginary, for between those elements which are capable
of an economic interpretation there subsist lacunae
or interworlds, which are occupied by myth. Myth is
not an ideology, that is to say, the veiling of an
economic reality which has to be uncovered but has
its proper function because these societies have not
yet broken the "umbilical cord" which ties them to
nature. It is this rupture which capitalist civilization
is destined to consummate and thereby the integration of a social system which, demystified or disen-
chanted, is organized as a capitalist economy and
thus into a single field of forces which from its own
momentum opens itself to an interpretation of its
unity which grasps it in its *truth*. Nevertheless, the
integration of society is checked by an internal im-
pediment: both in theory and in practice the system
fails to master the life of the social collectivity. In
order to escape a total judgment which it tends to
induce, capitalism poses itself as the eternal struc-

ture of the social world instead of a transitory phase in the social dynamic and the movement toward an objective understanding, which had laid the basis for a social consciousness, hardens into objectivism and scientism. This phase of social science is only an aspect of the general process of *reification* which separates capitalist civilization from its human origins and endows commodities and the laws of exchange in a market economy with a categorical value. In the proletariat Lukács discovers the class that is able to bring this sketch of society to its completion. Being in reality the extreme degree and absolute refusal of "reification," it is in fact and in principle "at the heart of the social process" and finds itself in a position to create and sustain a society that would genuinely be a transparent society, internally undivided and classless. With power in the hands of the proletariat, a system of production would be achieved which would not be shackled by its own forms, and would in turn provide the conditions for genuine knowledge of society and the whole of history.

The new society would outgrow the polemical concepts which it used in the struggle and, for example, Lukács specifies that historical materialism would change its function and meaning. In other words, the parallelism between economics and history, which in the capitalist stage of history meant that history was to be explained in terms of economics, in post-capitalist society would mean the equally

free development of unimpeded knowledge and production.

Despite the numerous questions raised by this
analysis, we are interested in it only from a metho-
dological standpoint inasmuch as it offers an image
of philosophy, or the quest for truth, as the concen-
tration of a meaning scattered through history or
outlined in it. There is no question of a philosophical reconstruction of history in terms of those provisional and abstracted frames of reference of which
Max Weber spoke, because what is involved is
the explanation of the movement of history through
the constitution within it of a class described as the
"suppression of itself" (*Selbstaufhebung*) and the
advent of the universal. Truth is not found in certain historical agents nor in the achievement of
theoretical consciousness, but in the confrontation
of the two, in their practice, and in their common
life. So conceived, history is the genesis of truth and
the "philosophy of history" is no longer a transcendental discipline but a coherent and total explication
of the meaning of human development, which of its
nature is essentially "philosophical." The circle of
existence to which Weber gave a theoretical formula, in his remark that man is a historian because
he is in history and because his practice is a call to
knowledge and theory, reappears in Lukács in the
form of a knowledge and practice which are solidary
and open. Thus Hegelian rationalism is put in question, for it is only afterwards, once human invention

has reintegrated them in the meaning of the totality, that the hazards of history can appear to be and are in fact rational without there being any place for the assumption of a hidden reason which orients them through the "ruse" of appearing in the guise of contingency. The logic of history imposes problems on the course of events and so long as they are not solved the contradictions accumulate and interact. But it does not of necessity impose any solution— the solution chosen by Lukács is only the incarnation of negativity in history, of the power of doubt and interrogation which Weber called "culture."

Can one continue to think that negativity remains identical once it has acquired a historical vehicle? It is all the more doubtful because Weber himself has renounced this position. Today, he emphasizes the opaqueness of social reality as a "second nature" and thus seems to postpone infinitely the limiting concept of transparent social relationships and therewith the categorical definition of history as the genesis of truth. This amounts to questioning the Marxist idea of a meaning which is imminent in history. This question should now be reopened.

5 / Institution in Personal and Public History

THE CONCEPT OF INSTITUTION may help us to find a solution to certain difficulties in the philosophy of consciousness. For consciousness there are only the objects which it has itself constituted. Even if it is granted that certain of the objects are "never completely" so (Husserl), they are at each moment the exact reflection of the activity and faculties of consciousness. There is nothing in the objects capable of throwing consciousness back toward other perspectives. There is no exchange, no interaction between consciousness and the object. When consciousness considers its own past, all that it knows is that for a long time there has been this other, mysteriously called me, but with whom I have nothing in common except an absolutely universal ipseity which I share just as much with every "other" of whom I can form a concept. My past has yielded to my present by means of a series of fragmentations.

Finally, when consciousness considers others, their existence only means the negation of itself; it does not know that they behold it, it only knows that it is beheld. Different times and diverse temporalities are incompossible and merely form a system of reciprocal exclusions.

If the subject were taken not as a constituting but an instituting subject, it might be understood that the subject does not exist instantaneously and that the other person does not exist simply as a negative of myself. What I have begun at certain decisive moments would exist neither far off in the past as an objective memory nor be present like a memory revived, but really between the two as the field of my becoming during that period. Likewise my relation to another person would not be reducible to a disjunction: an instituting subject could coexist with another because the one instituted is not the immediate reflection of the activity of the former and can be regained by himself or by others without involving anything like a total recreation. Thus the instituted subject exists between others and myself, between me and myself, like a hinge, the consequence and the guarantee of our belonging to a common world.

Thus what we understand by the concept of institution are those events in experience which endow it with durable dimensions, in relation to which a whole series of other experiences will acquire meaning, will form an intelligible series or a history—or again those events which sediment in me a meaning, not just as survivals or residues, but as the invitation to a sequel, the necessity of a future.

The concept of institution has been approached through four different levels of phenomena, of which the first three deal with personal or inter-subjective history and the last with public history.

There exists something comparable to institu-tion even at the animal level (the animal is impreg-nated by the living creatures which surround him at birth)—and even at the level of human functions which used to be considered purely "biological" (puberty reveals a conservation rhythm—the recall and transcendence of earlier events—relevant here is the oedipal conflict—which is characteristic of institution). However, in man the past is able not only to orient the future or to furnish the frame of reference for the problems of the adult person, but beyond that to give rise to a *search,* in the manner of Kafka, or to an indefinite elaboration: in this case conservation and transcendence are more profound, so that it becomes impossible to explain behavior in terms of its past, anymore than in terms of its future. The analysis of love in Proust reveals this "simultaneity," this crystallization upon each other of the past and the future, of subject and "object," of the positive and the negative. At first approxima-tion, sentiment is an illusion and its institution a habit, since it involves a transference of a way of loving learned elsewhere or in childhood. It is a kind of love which never holds for anything but an inte-rior image of the "object," and for such a love to be true and to really reach the other person it would be necessary that it had never been lived by anyone. However, once it has been recognized that pure love is impossible and that it would be a pure negation, it remains to establish that this negation is a fact, that this impossibility has happened. Thus Proust envisages a *via negativa* of love, manifest beyond any question in the experience of chagrin, despite the fact that the latter is the reality of separation and jealousy. At the highest point of alienation, jealousy becomes disinterestedness; it is quite impossible to pretend that a present love is nothing but a reverberation of the past. On the contrary, the past takes on the outline of a preparation or premeditation of a present that exceeds it in meaning although it recognizes itself in it.

The institution of a painter's work, or of a style in the history of painting, reveals the same subterranean logic. A painter learns to paint other than by imitating his predecessors. Each of his works announces those to follow—and makes it so that they cannot be the same. Everything hangs together, and yet he cannot say in which direction he is going. Likewise, in the history of painting, problems (such as that of perspective, for example) are rarely resolved directly. The search halts at an impasse, other inquiries seem to create a diversion, but the new thrust seems to enable the obstacle to be overcome from another direction. Thus, rather than a *problem*, there is an "interrogation" of painting,

which lends a common significance to all its endeav-
ors and binds them into a history, but never such
that it can be anticipated conceptually.

Is all this true merely of the preobjective domain
of personal life and art? Is there, in the development of knowledge, a manifest logic to which
knowledge conforms? If there is such a truth, should
not the truths be coordinated in a system which
only gradually reveals itself, but whose entirety re-
sides in itself outside of time? In order to be more
agile and apparently more free, the development of
knowledge manifests the same internal circulation
between the past and present which has been ob-
served in other institutions. The series of "idealiza-
tions" which reveals the whole number as a special
case of a more essential number does not land us in
an intelligible world from which it might be de-
duced; rather it resumes the evidence proper to the
whole number, which remains understood. The historicity of knowledge is not an "apparent" characteristic of knowledge which would leave us free to
define truth "in itself" analytically. Even in the order
of exact knowledge what is held is a "structural"
conception of truth (Wertheimer). Truth exists in
the sense of a field common to the diverse enter-
prises of knowledge.

If theoretical consciousness, in its most assured
forms, is not free from historicity, one might think
that in return history would benefit from a *rap-
prochement* with theory and, with the preceding

restrictions concerning the notion of system, allow itself to be dominated by thought. This would be to overlook that thought only has access to another historical horizon, to another "mental toolbox" (L. Febvre) through the self-criticism of its categories, through a lateral penetration and not by a sort of ubiquity in principle. There occurs a simultaneous decentering and recentering of the elements in our personal life, a movement by us toward the past and of the reanimated past toward us. Now this working of the past against the present does not culminate in a closed universal history or a complete system of all the possible human combinations with respect to such an institution as, for example, kinship. Rather, it produces a table of diverse, complex probabilities, always bound to local circumstances, weighted with a coefficient of facticity, and such that we can never say of one that it is more true than another, although we can say that one is more false, more artificial, and less open to a future in turn less rich.

These fragmentary analyses are intended as a revision of Hegelianism, which is the discovery of phenomenology, of the living, real and original relation between the elements of the world. But Hegelianism situates this relation in the past in order to subordinate it to the systematic vision of the philosopher. Now phenomenology is either nothing but an introduction to absolute knowledge, which remains a stranger to the adventures of experience, or phenomenology dwells entirely within philosophy; it cannot conclude with the predialectical formula that "being exists" and it has to take into account the mediation of being. It is this development of phenomenology into a metaphysics of history that we wished to outline here.

6 / The Problem of Passivity: Sleep, the Unconscious, Memory

How can we imagine that there is a subject which never encounters obstacles? If the subject has created the obstacles itself, then they are not obstacles. But if they really do offer resistance to the subject, then we are brought back to the difficulties of a philosophy which incorporates the subject in a cosmic order and treats the operation of spirit as a particular case of natural finality.

Every theory of perception runs into this problem, and thus an explication of perceptual experience should oblige us to become acquainted with a kind of being over which the subject is not sovereign and yet not enclosed within it.

In this course we have attempted to develop an ontology of the perceived world going beyond sensible nature. Whether we are trying to understand how consciousness can sleep, how it can be inspired by a past which it has apparently lost, or finally how it can open up again to that past, it is possible to speak of passivity only on the condition that "to be conscious" does not mean "to give a meaning," which one projects onto an ungraspable object of knowledge, but to realize a certain distance, a certain variation in a field of existence already instituted, which is always behind us and whose weight, like that of an object in flight, only intervenes in the actions by which we transform it. For man, to live is not simply to be constantly conferring meaning upon things but to continue a vortex of experience which was set up at our birth, at the point of contact between the "outside" and he who is called to live it.

Despite the words, sleep is not an act, the operation, the thought, or the consciousness of sleeping; sleep is a modality of perceptual activity—more precisely, it is the provisional involution or differentiation of the latter. Sleep is the return to the inarticulated, the resort to a global or prepersonal relation to the world—which is not really absent but is, rather, distant—in which our place is marked by the body with which a minimum of contact is maintained that makes it possible to wake up. A philosophy of consciousness translates—and distorts—this relation by postulating that sleep consists in being absent from the real world or being present in an imaginary world without any consistency, which is to explain the negative in terms of the positive in the absence of any criteria or controls. The negation of the world in sleep is equally a way of upholding it, and thus sleeping consciousness is not a recess of pure nothingness: it is cluttered with the debris of the past and present; it plays among it.

A dream is not simply a variety of conscious imagination as it operates in waking states, namely, as a pure power of envisaging anything at all in any symbol whatsoever. If a dream were just this unlimited caprice, surrendering consciousness to its essential folly, which comes from having no substance and of becoming immediately what it invents or thinks it is, then it is difficult to see how consciousness once asleep could ever awaken, how it could ever take seriously the conditions in which awakening is an affirmation of reality, or how our dreams could have the sort of weight they have for us, which they owe to their relation with our past. The distinction between the real and the oneiric cannot be identical with the simple distinction between consciousness filled by meaning and consciousness given up to its own void. The two modalities impinge upon one another. Our waking relations with objects and others especially have an oneiric character as a matter of principle: others are present to us in the way that dreams are, the way myths are, and this is enough to question the cleavage between the real and the imaginary.

The discussion of dreams already raises the problem of the unconscious, the refuge of the subject in dream, of that which dreams in us, of the inexhaustible, indestructible fund from which our dreams are drawn. Freud has been rightly criticized for having introduced under the name of the unconscious a second thinking subject whose creations are simply received by the first, and he himself has admitted that this "demonology" was only a "misbegotten psychological conception." But discussion of the Freudian unconscious usually leads to a monopoly of consciousness: the unconscious is reduced to what we decide not to assume, and, since this decision presupposes that we are in contact with the repressed, the unconscious proves to be nothing more than a particular instance of bad faith, a hesitation of imaginative freedom. Such a view loses sight of what was Freud's most interesting insight —not the idea of a second "I think" which could know what we do not know about ourselves—but the idea of a symbolism which is primordial, originary, the idea of a "non-conventional thought" (Politzer) enclosed in a "world for us," which is the source of dreams and more generally of the elaboration of our life. To dream is not to translate a latent content, which is clear to itself (or to the second thinking subject), into the equally clear but deceiving language of manifest content. That would not be its "adequate" expression from the standpoint of awakened thought, without for that reason being its deliberate concealment. For the language of manifest content is *valid for* the latent content in virtue of certain equivalences, certain modes of projection called forth by the primordial symbolism and the structure of oneiric consciousness. In Freud's *Science of Dreams* there is a complete description of oneiric consciousness—the consciousness which ig-

nores the *no,* which only says *yes* tacitly, producing
for the analyst the responses he was expecting from
it, being incapable of speech, calculation and real
thoughts, and thus reduced to the subject's ancient
elaborations, so that our dreams are not circumscribed the moment we dream them, but import *en
bloc* into our present whole fragments of our previous duration. What these descriptions mean is
that the unconscious is a perceiving consciousness
and that it operates as such through a logic of implication or promiscuity, follows closer and closer a
path whose slope it cannot see clearly, and envisages objects and creatures through the negative that
it withholds, which suffices to regulate its steps
without enabling it to name them "by their name."
Like the dream, delirium is full of immanent truths
and moves through a network of relations equiva-
lent to true relations of which it lacks possession yet
takes into account. Freud's contribution is not to
have revealed quite another reality beneath appearances, but that the analysis of given behavior always discovers several layers of signification, each
with its own truth, and that the plurality of possible
interpretations is the discursive expression of a
mixed life in which every choice always has several
meanings, it being impossible to say which of them
is the only true one.

The problem of memory remains a dead end as
long as one hesitates between the conceptions of
memory as conservation and memory as construction. It is always possible to show that conscious-

ness only finds in its "representations" what it has put into them, and thus that memory is construction —and that nevertheless another memory behind the latter is needed to measure the value of its creations, in other words, a past given gratuitously and in a way quite opposite to the operation of memory as construction. Only if we abandon the description of the problem in terms of "representation" can we reconcile the immanence and transcendence of the past, the activity and passivity of memory. Instead of a "representation" (*Vorstellung*), we might begin by viewing the present as a certain unique position of the index of being-in-the-world, and our relations with the present when the present slips into the past, like our relations with our surroundings, might be attributed to a postural schema which unfolds and shapes a series of positions and temporal possibilities, so that the body could be regarded as that which answers each time to the question "Where am I and what time is it?" Then there would be no question of any alternative between conservation and construction; memory would not be the opposite of forgetfulness, and it might be seen that true memory is to be found at the intersection of the two, at the moment where memory forgotten and kept by forgetfulness returns. It might then be clear that forgetfulness and memory recalled are two modes of our oblique relation with a past that is present to us only through the determinate void that it leaves in us.

These phenomenological descriptions are always

somewhat misleading because they limit themselves to unraveling the negative in the positive and the positive in the negative. Reflection seems to demand supplementary clarification. Description will only have its full import when one begins to question oneself about the foundations of this need itself and gives reasons why in principle the relations between the positive and the negative present themselves as they do, which is to lay the foundations of a dialectical philosophy.

7 / Dialectical Philosophy

THE VERY TITLE OF THIS COURSE assumes the existence of a mode of thinking which, despite their differences, is common to so-called "dialectical" philosophers. There is no question of justifying this idea by the methods of inductive history. However, neither is it a matter of *replacing* the conclusions of history (supposing history could ever be conclusive) with a model. We propose simply to circumscribe a mode of thought and to sketch certain themes, which are as relevant today as they were yesterday. The various philosophies from the past are introduced—particularly in Monday's course [1]—solely to lend a voice to this schema. This analysis is intended to reclaim philosophy's right simply to reflect upon its past, to rediscover itself within it. In its place this is a legitimate exercise

1. "Texts and Commentaries on the Dialectic," pp. 60–61 below.—*Trans.*

within the history of philosophy. It is all the more so even if it limits itself to what past philosophies *could have meant,* taking into account their historical context, their internal structure, and their explicit problems.

Dialectical thought has been defined as follows:

[1] DIALECTIC OF CONTRADICTORIES

This means a dialectic which does not admit between contradictory terms either the relativist reconciliation or that identification through equivocation played upon by the "bad dialectic." If each of the opposed terms is nothing but the absence or the impossibility of the other, then they call for each other to the degree that they exclude one another and so pass in continual succession before a mind which is never able to posit them. An effective contradiction exists only where the relation between the positive and the negative is not one of alternation, but where the negation of the negation is capable of exercising its function against itself as an abstract or immediate negation and so founding contradiction while founding its transcendence. The Hegelian notion of the *negation of the negation* is not a solution of despair, nor is it a verbal artifice to escape from embarrassment. It is the formula of every operative contradiction and by leaving it aside one abandons dialectical thought itself, which is the fecundity of contradiction. The notion of a labor of the negative, as a negation which neither exhausts itself in the exclusion of the positive nor, when confronted with it, exhausts itself in conjuring up a term which annuls it, but instead reconstructs the positive beyond its limitations, destroying it and preserving it, is not a gradual perfecting or sclerosis of dialectical thought: it is its primordial resort (moreover, it is not astonishing to find it intimated in Plato where he calls the "same" the "other than the other"). We have related the notion of negation to the modern notion of *transcendence*, that is to say, to a being which is in principle at a distance, in regard to which distance is a bond but with which there can be no question of coincidence. Here, as in the other case, the relation of self to self passes through the external, the immediate demands mediation, or, again, mediation exists through the self.

[2] "SUBJECTIVE" DIALECTIC

Dialectical thought developed after the philosophy of reflection and in a sense is its adversary since it conceives its own beginning as a problem, whereas the philosophy of reflection reduces the unreflected, as a simple absence, to the meaning which reflection thereafter discovers in it. However, one can say that the dialectic is "subjective" reflection in the sense understood by Kierkegaard or Heidegger, namely, that it does not make being rest upon itself but makes it appear before someone as the response to an interrogation. It is not simply a question, as someone has said, of "relativizing subject and object." Like all "relativist" thought this remark limits itself to handling the common life of the opposed terms by reducing contradiction to a difference in relations. But it will not suffice to say vaguely that the object is subjectivity in a certain relation and subjectivity is object in another relation. It is by means of what is most negative within subjectivity that it needs a world and by means of what is most positive within it that being needs non-being in order to circumscribe and delimit being. Thus dialectical thought invites us to revise the ordinary notions of subject and object.

[3] CIRCULAR DIALECTIC

Because dialectical thought is unwilling to sacrifice to the other either reflection or the unreflected it sees itself as the simultaneous development and destruction of that which preceded it and thus its conclusions retain the whole progression by which they were achieved. In truth, the dialectical conclusion is only the integration of the preceding advances. The dialectician is thus a perpetual beginner. That is to say, the circularity of dialectical thought is not that of a reflection which has made all the rounds and found nothing new to reflect upon. On the contrary, truth would cease to be an operative truth if it were to separate itself from its own development, or to forget it or really to put it in the past; and so everything has always to be re-thought in the dialectic. It is therefore no accident that in the nineteenth century the dialectic was "applied" to history and that in this field the dialectic simply comes into its own. For it is essential to it to realize itself only gradually, to move on and never express itself, as Hegel says, "in a single proposition." Already in Plato, as is shown by the famous "parricide" in the *Parmenides,* the notion of genesis or historical filiation is included among those negations which interiorize and conserve and is regarded as a principal example of a dialectical relation. Finally, although here again Hegel only provided the formula, the dialectic has always been conceived as an *experience* of thought, in other words, a journey in the course of which it learns, even though what it learns was already there, "in itself," before reflection which is only its passage to being for itself.

Understood in this way, dialectical thought is an uneasy equilibrium. As negative thought, it contains an element of transcendence and is unable to limit itself to the relation of multiplicity but is open, as Plato said, to an ἐπέκεινα τῆς οὐσίας. But, furthermore, this transcendence of being, whose source remains fixed, unlike the One of the First Hypothesis in the *Parmenides,* can be neither thought nor being and always appears only through a plural participation. There is therefore a dialectical absolute solely for the sake of maintaining the position and contours of the multiple and to oppose the absolutization of relations. It is "fluidified" in them and it is immanent to experience. This is a position which is unstable by definition and is always threatened either by positivist or negativist thought.

In the latter part of the course, we propose to study some of these deviations. In Hegel we examined the transition of the dialectic to speculation, of the "negatively rational" to the "positively rational," which finally transforms the dialectic into a system. And in the definition of the absolute we saw the balance swing in favor of the subject which thus gives an ontological priority to "interiority" and in particular dispossesses nature of its own concept, making exteriority a "feebleness of nature." All the same, the critique of system and speculation in Hegel's successors does not constitute a genuine return to dialectical inspiration. In Kierkegaard, the polemic against "objective" and "world historical" thought is sane in itself and might have initiated a concrete dialectic. But it ends in an attack on mediation, which is to say dialectical thought itself, and with an endorsement, under the singular name of "decision" or "choice," of the task of distinction between contradictories, a faith determined by its ignorance, a joy defined by its suffering, a sort of "religious atheism." In Marx at the time of the 1844 Manuscript,[2] alongside a conception of history as

2. Karl Marx, *Economic and Philosophical Manuscripts of 1844*, ed. D. Struik, trans. M. Milligan (New York: International Publishers, n.d.).—*Trans.*

man's "act of birth" and as negativity, which he defends against Feuerbach, we found a naturalist philosophy which localizes the dialectic in the pre-paratory phase of human "prehistory" and assumes as its horizon, beyond communism, as the "negation of the negation," the wholly positive life of man as a "natural" or "objective" being which is the resolution of the enigma of history. The latter philosophy is definitely predominant in *Capital* (that is why Marx could there define the dialectic as "the positive intel-ligence of things as they exist") and much more so among Marxists. Among our contemporaries it is again "negativist" thought which is dominant and curiously colors their neo-Marxism. In Sartre there can be no dialectic between the being which is wholly positive and nothingness which "is not." What takes its place is a sort of sacrifice of nothing-ness which devotes itself entirely to the manifesta-tion of being and negates absolutely the absolute negation that it is itself. Being at once master and servant, negation and negated, the negative is equiv-ocal in principle: its loyalty is a refusal, its refusal a loyalty. In the order of being to which the negative is a stranger, it is unable to find a criterion for its choices. For, in founding a choice, a criterion would subject negation to conditions and there are no con-ditions which guarantee and limit the relation of being to nothingness. This relation is, so to speak, total or null; it is total because nothingness is not and it is not nothing because it demands totality.

Sartre's is a philosophy which manifests, more than any other has done, the crisis, the essential difficulty, and the task of the dialectic.

[4] TEXTS AND COMMENTARIES
ON THE DIALECTIC

This course was planned as a free commentary upon texts chosen within as well as outside dialectical philosophy for the light that they throw upon dialectical thought.

Zeno's arguments have been studied as a sort of test of dialectical thought by each generation of philosophers who have discussed them. At first considered (and by Bergson still) as *sophisms* to which a direct intuition must do justice, they were finally recognized as paradoxes characteristic of the mathematical relations between the finite and the infinite (A. Koyré). The legend of Zeno illustrates the transition of a thought which denounces logical scandals in the name of an ideal of identity to a thought which on the contrary welcomes contradiction as the movement of being, a transition from a garrulous and "ventriloquist" dialectic to the real dialectic.

Plato's *Parmenides*, as well as the *Theaetetus* and the *Sophist*, have been studied as examples of a thought which is neither ascendant nor descendant, which, so to speak, keeps its place. This served as an opportunity to discuss recent interpretations of dualism and decadence in Plato.

We then went on to note traces of the dialectic in authors who make no profession of it but harbor it unwittingly or even against their will. Such is the case with Montaigne, in whom it is, above all, the description of the paradoxes of the self and of the rare occasions, which constitute its wisdom, where we succeed in getting the whole of our being "to work in a single unity." Likewise Descartes, whose principle of the "order of reasons" offers us the least dialectical philosophy there ever was, but who found himself led to envisage an order which would not necessarily be linear and to suggest a *nexus rationum*. Finally, we saw the same in Pascal when he sketched a method of convergence and a conception of "order" which is quasi-perceptual, with digression and return to a center, which is to say, a dialectical theory of truth.

The transition from Kant's *Antinomy of Pure Reason* to Hegel's dialectic—described by M. Gueroult in his article of 1931 [3]—offered the occasion for a re-examination of the relation of philosophy to history and the history of philosophy as an exercise in dialectical thought.

3. Martial Gueroult, "Le Jugement de Hegel sur l'antithétique de la raison pure," *Revue de métaphysique et de morale,* 1931, pp. 413–39.—*Trans.*

IN TAKING THE CONCEPT OF NATURE as the sole topic of this year's course, as well as next, we may seem to be stressing an unreal problem. But the neglect which has fallen upon the philosophy of nature embraces also a certain conception of spirit, history and man, namely, the assumption of making them appear as pure negativity. By contrast, in returning to the philosophy of nature, we only seem to be looking away from these fundamental problems; in fact, we are trying to lay the ground for a solution to them which is not *immaterialist*. Naturalism apart, an ontology which leaves nature in silence shuts itself in the incorporeal and for this very reason gives a fantastic image of man, spirit and history. If we have stressed the problem of nature, it is from the double conviction that it cannot by itself solve the ontological problem but that neither is it a subordinate or secondary element in any such solution.

At first sight it is astounding that Marxist philosophers have given so little attention to this problem, which should be their special concern. The concept of nature makes only brief and fleeting appearances in their works. It appears there only to attest that we are not in the in-itself, in an opaque being, a pure object. Yet what do we know about nature which allows us to assign it this ontological role? The question is not raised. The certitude of being in principle in the "objective" authorizes great inattention to its implications and numerous abstract constructions with respect to our knowledge of nature and matter. This poor dialectic has its origins perhaps in Marx himself. In the *Economic and Philosophic Manuscripts, 1844* nature is described on the one hand as a state of equilibrium existing in its own right—the stable being which will again close in upon human history at its end—and on the other hand as that which human history negates and transforms. Instead of being mastered or transcended, these two conceptions are simply juxtaposed, and finally forced to mix in the absolute of "objective activity" (*Theses on Feuerbach*): Thus it is possible that Marx's own philosophy presupposes a quite objectivist concept of nature, in order at times to affirm, and at others to negate nature. The result is always the same; even when a Marxist philosopher (G. Lukács) admits that Marxism cannot simply endorse Feuerbach's naturalism against Hegel's idealism, he nevertheless does not risk describing the third position, the true *medium* of the dialectic, but proceeds without further specification to a profession of "materialism."[1] With all the more reason, everyone avoids any confrontation between Engels' conception of nature and that which we have come to know in the last fifty years. The most famous of all philosophies of history rests upon a concept which has never been elucidated and which may be mythical. As a pure object, or being in itself, which contains everything that exists and yet is not to be found in human experience since from the very beginning man shapes and transforms it, nature in the Marxist philosophy of history is everywhere and nowhere, like a visitation. In trying to elucidate this problem, we are threfore not so far from history.

In truth, as soon as one probes into it a little, one encounters an enigma in which the subject, spirit, history and the whole of philosophy are involved. For nature is not simply the object, the accessory of consciousness in its tête-à-tête with knowledge. It is an object from which we have arisen, in which our beginnings have been posited little by little until the very moment of tying themselves to an existence which they continue to sustain and aliment. Whether in the case of the individual event of birth, or the birth of institutions and societies, the originary relation between man and being is not that of the for-itself to the in-itself, for this relation occurs in each man capable of perception. However surcharged with historical significations man's perception may be, it borrows from the primordial at least its manner of presenting the object and its ambiguous evidence. Nature, says Lucien Herr in a comment upon Hegel, "is there from the first day." It presents itself always as already there before us, and yet as new before our gaze. Reflexive thought is disoriented by this implication of the immemorial in the present, the appeal from the past to the most recent present. For reflexive thought each fragment of space exists on its own account and they can only coexist under its gaze and through its activity; each moment of the world ceases to exist when it ceases to be present and is only held in past being by reflexive thought. If it were possible to abolish in thought all individual consciousness there would remain only a flash of instantaneous being, extinguished no sooner than it has appeared. The phantom and tenacious existence of the past is converted into a posited being, which may be clear or confused, empty or full, but in any case is the exact correlative of our acts of knowing. All that is to be found at the limits of the spirit is *mens momentanea seu recordiatione carens*, that is to say, ultimately, nothing. If we are not to be resigned to saying that a world from which consciousness is cut off is nothing at all, then in some way we must recognize that primordial being which is not yet the subject-being nor the object-being and which in every respect baffles reflection. From this primordial being to us, there is no derivation, nor any break; it has neither the tight construction of the mechanism nor the transparency of a whole which precedes its parts. We can neither conceive of primordial being engendering itself, which would make it infinite, nor think of it being engendered by another, which would reduce it to the condition of a product and a dead result. As Schelling has remarked, there is in nature something which makes it such that it would impose itself upon God himself as an independent condition of his operation. Such is our problem.

Before trying to solve this problem, it was necessary to rediscover it in different traditions of thought. We have decided to begin, in this year's course, with a survey of the historical elements in our concept of nature. It is only following this that we begin to seek in the development of knowledge the symptoms of a new conception of nature. This task could only be undertaken this year with respect to physical nature. Next year we shall continue with the examination of the conception of life and culture to be found in contemporary research. Once this is done, we shall be in a position to ascertain the philosophical signification of the concept of nature.

[1] ELEMENTS OF OUR CONCEPT OF NATURE

1.

Since our aim is not to construct a history of the concept of nature, the pre-Cartesian conceptions of nature as a destiny or total dynamic of which man is a part have not been studied in their own right. It seemed preferable to take as a reference-point a "Cartesian" conception which, rightly or wrongly, still overhangs contemporary ideas about nature— which is likely to raise pre-Cartesian themes that remain alive long after Descartes.

2. *The Cartesian Idea of Nature*

Descartes admits that, even if God had created our world all at once with the structure that it has, the immanent play of the laws of nature would have imposed themselves upon Him and the same act since these laws stem of necessity from the attributes of finite being. This implies the reduction of the facticity of nature to its bare existence. Thus, the world might not have existed, had God not decided to create it; it therefore arose from a "before" in which nothing or no preponderant possibility prefigured it or called it into existence. But, once the world has arisen, it is necessitated to be such as we see it; it is what it is without hesitation, without error, without weakness; its reality contains no fault or fissure. The alternative of the world's nonexistence, which remains possible if we take God's view of things, in no way deprives it of its solidity. On the contrary, this alternative acknowledges the world's solidity because it makes it understood that, if the world were not such as we see it, it would not exist at all. God's being is defined by the same dilemma: to say that he is the cause of himself is to try to imagine that which is nothing and to maintain that, on this ground, one sees the emergence of a being who takes off and produces himself. The hypothesis of the Nothing, which had its truth with respect to the world, is in the latter case purely verbal: there has never been any possibility that God does not exist. It is however a hypothesis at the horizon of Descartes' thought: "cause of itself" would be meaningless if one were not to evoke for a moment, even fictionally, a God *effect*, which, like every effect, needs to be sustained by its cause and could not exist without it. Human beings are not able to think that which is nothing, they are surrounded by an infinite plenitude; when they set about thinking, the die is already cast: to think, it is necessary to be. Nevertheless, thought only recognizes itself at the highest point of doubt, in the moment where thought of its own accord denies everything that is. In the same manner, that which is cause of itself is only found through the dependence of all existing things, and the power with which it sustains its own existence is exactly proportionate to the hesitation which it ends.

Such is the ontological complex in which we find

the Cartesian concept of nature. It obliges every being, under pain of being nothing, to exist completely without hiatus, and with no hidden possibilities. There is to be nothing occult or enveloped in nature any more. Nature must be a mechanism and one should be able in principle to derive the form of this world from laws which are themselves the expression of the internal force of infinite production. In accordance with a distinction drawn long before Descartes but reinvigorated by his reflections, what we call nature is a *naturata*, a pure product, composed of absolutely external parts, completely existent and clearly combined—an "empty shell," as Hegel would say. Everything internal is handed over to God's side, the pure *naturans*. Both historically and philosophically our idea of natural being *qua* object in itself, which is what it is because it cannot be another thing, derives from the idea of an unlimited being, infinite or *causa sui*, and this in turn comes from the alternation between being and nothing. The Cartesian conception of nature will outlive this ontology, enduring as the common stock of scientists who continue to struggle to bring their own achievements within its jurisdiction until the quite un-Cartesian developments in contemporary science open up for them a different ontology.

Yet, even without going beyond Descartes' writings, one might have recognized the limitations of his ontology. For the concept of nature that we have referred to is in fact that which reveals to us its essence as evident, nature according to the *lumen naturale*. But, by maintaining the contingency of the act of creation, Descartes upheld the facticity of nature and thus legitimated another perspective on this existent nature than that of pure understanding. To this nature we have an access, not only through it, but through the vital relation that we have with a privileged part of nature: namely, our body, through the "natural inclination" whose lessons cannot coincide with those of pure understanding. It is life which validly comprehends the life of the human composite. But how can we leave the definition of being and truth to pure understanding if it is not grounded so as to know the existent world? Moreover, if we take into account the definition of space, for example, the space of our body with which we are united substantially, how can we maintain the definition of the extended object given to the understanding? Descartes' hesitations in the theory of the human body are witness to this difficulty. His position seems to be that for us the experience of existence is irreducible to the view of it in pure understanding, yet experience cannot teach us anything which might be contrary to understanding, and is not in itself—that is to say, for God—incompatible with understanding and his will: if nature exists only through the decision—and the continuing decision—of God, then it does not "hold" in time (nor for that matter in space) by necessity of its own fundamental laws. Nature as event or an ensemble of events remains different from nature as object, or an ensemble of objects, as does God conceived as the free creator of the world and God as the source of a causality from which derives an eminently finitized world.

3. *Kantian Humanism and Nature*

Kantianism abandons the derivation of natural being as the only possible manifestation of infinite being—but not in order to acknowledge it as brute being and to undertake its study. Such a study is declined in the *Critique of Pure Reason* by defining nature as "the sum of meaningful objects" (*Inbegriff der Gegenstände der Sinne*) coordinated under the *Naturbegriffe* of the human understanding. We can only speak of a nature that is nature for us; in this regard nature remains the object which Descartes had in mind, it is an object constructed by us.

However, Kant goes beyond this anthropological philosophy. The organism, in which every event is cause and effect of all the others, and in this sense cause of itself, raises the problem of an auto-production of the whole, or, more precisely, of a totality which, in contrast with human technique, works upon materials which are its very own and, so to speak, emanates from them. It seems that within an entity that is in the world one encounters a mode of liaison which is not the connection of external causality, that is, an "interior" unlike the interior of consciousness, and thus nature must be something other than an object. We need not wait, says Kant, for another Newton to help us understand by means of causal relations what a blade of grass is. How are we to ground these natural totalities? Are we to say that we must uphold in juxtaposition, as two aspects of human consciousness, both the order of causal explanation and the order of totality? Would we then hold that when localized in phenomena (with every reservation with respect to the things in themselves) these two modes of apprehension are equally legitimate and compatible? But the retreat to the human order of phenomena evokes by definition an order of things themselves in which diverse human perspectives are impossible, since all of them together are real. In order for causal explanation and the perception of the totality to be in principle equally legitimate, it is not sufficient to claim that both causality and totality are as dogma equally false. Both have to be considered true of objects and false only when held in exclusion of one another. The idea of a discursive understanding with the authority to order our experience, though confined to this task, implies at least the idea of a "non-discursive understanding" that would ground simultaneously the possibility of causal explication and the perception of totality. The philosophy of human representation is not false, it is superficial. It assumes a reconciliation of thesis and antithesis for which man is the theater but not the agent.

In the last analysis, Kant does not take this path, which was taken later by Romantic philosophy. Although he anticipated Schelling in his description of the enigma of an organic totality, of a natural production in which both form and materials have a common origin and thereby controvert any analogy with human technique, Kant definitely considers the "natural end" (*Naturzweck*) as merely an anthropological term, though legitimate enough. Reflections upon totality are inevitable in every human subject, since they express the pleasure we experience in establishing a spontaneous accord between the contingency of what exists and the legislation of the understanding. They in no way designate anything constitutive of natural being, but are simply the happy encounter of our faculties. Nature, as a sum of "meaningful objects," is defined in terms of the *Naturbegriffe* of Newtonian physics. We think about it much more in its own way, but these are only reflections of ours. If we wished to realize them as properties of the thing itself we should be prevented by the manifest failures of teleology. The consideration of nature from this standpoint would yield at best a "demonology." It is in the "concept of freedom" only and consequently in consciousness and man that the conformity of the elements to a concept takes on a real sense, so that the teleology of nature is a reflection of "noumenal man." The truth of teleology is the consciousness of freedom. Man is the only goal of nature, not because nature prepares him and creates him, but because man retroactively confers upon nature an air of finality by positing its autonomy.

The reappearance of Kantianism in the nineteenth century represents the victory of this anthropological philosophy over the philosophy of nature that Kant had envisaged and his successors had wished to develop. Léon Braunschvicg thought he could salvage the best in Kant by effacing the *a priori* structure of the understanding and the facticity of experience which was the motive in Kant for the ideal of an intuitive understanding. He treated the radical originality of natural being as an enigma. But the remedy only aggravates the ill. If, as Braunschvicg says, we no longer have the right to speak of an architectonic of nature, if the concepts of the understanding share in the contingency of experience and are always weighted by a "coefficient of facticity" which ties them to specific structures of the world, should our laws have no meaning except on the supposition of certain synchronisms of which they are not the source but merely an expression, and finally if there is, as the Stoics foresaw, a brute unity through which the universe "holds" and of which the unity of human understanding is the expression rather than the internal condition, then the being of nature is decidedly not its object-being and there reappears the problem of a philosophy of nature.

4. Essays on the Philosophy of Nature

The Cartesian conception of necessary being was overtly questioned by Schelling. To him, as for Kant, it was "the abyss of human reason." Necessary being could not be primary unless it was able to put itself in question. But, if it does so and raises, as Kant says, the question "Where am I?" it disqualifies itself as the primary being. Reflection cannot closet itself and withdraw into the idea of necessary being. But, whereas Kant abandons the idea as unknowable and mistaken (eventually to fall into a metaphysic of the subject), Schelling considers the "abyss" itself to be an ultimate reality and defines the absolute as that which exists without reason (*grundlos*), as the "over-being" who sustains the "grand fact of the world." Just as the absolute is no longer its own cause, or the absolute antithesis of nothingness, so nature no longer possesses the absolute positivity of "the only possible world." The *erste Natur* is an ambiguous principle, or, as he puts it, a "barbarous" principle which can be transcended, but will never be as though it had never existed, and can never be considered secondary even in relation to God. With all the more reason, can there be no question of explaining the enigma of natural production by our faculty of judgment or human reflection. "What Kant, at the end of his sober discourse, one day dreamed virtually," Schelling tries to think, or rather live (*leben*) and experience (*erleben*). What we have here is the "intellectual intuition," which is not an occult faculty, but perception as it is before it has been reduced to ideas; it is perception dormant within itself, in which all things are me because I am not yet the reflecting subject. At this level, light and air are not yet, as in Fichte, the milieu of vision and hearing, the means whereby rational creatures communicate, but "the symbols of an eternal and originary knowledge (*Urwissen*) inscribed in Nature." *Urwissen* is a bound and silent knowledge brought into being by man alone yet obliging us to say that man is the conscious development of the natural production, he who becomes nature is distancing himself from nature in order to learn about it. In principle (one cannot say as much for the poets and writers around him—nor even for the evil genius in Schelling which distracted him from his principles), nature in Schelling never gives rise to a second science or a gnosis which would objectivate and absurdly convert into a second causality the relations of existing nature as we glimpse them in the "ek-stasis" of intellectual intuition. There is only the effort to take account of the weight of the existing world, to make of nature something else than an "impotency" (Hegel) and an absence of the concept. Lukács [2] gives Schelling the honor of having introduced "the doctrine of the reflection (*Wiederspiegelung*) into transcendental philosophy," but regrets that he gave it an "idealist" and "mystic" twist. What Lukács considers irrational is doubtless the idea of an exchange between nature and consciousness within man, an internal relation between man and nature. It is clear, however, that the "doctrine of the reflection," or the mirror, leaves nature in the state of an *object* which we reflect, and that, if philosophy is to avoid immaterialism, it

2. Georg Lukács, *Die Zerstörung der Vernunft* (Berlin: Aufbau, 1955), p. 110.

must establish a more strict relation between man and nature than this looking-glass relation, since nature and consciousness can only truly communicate in us and through our incarnate being. And this is a relation which neither suppresses nor replaces the relation we have so richly with the human milieu of history; it merely invites us to conceive it in its turn as an effective contact, instead of construing it also as a "reflection" of a process which is historical in itself.

Bergson might seem to be far removed from what is best in Schelling. Bergson, unlike Schelling, does not seek the unreflected in a doubling of reflection ("intuition," as the young Hegel put it). He seems to take his stand wholly within the positive, and if he is dislodged from it in the course of his analysis it is as though despite himself and in complete unconsciousness of such a dialectic. Nevertheless there is enough substance in this criticism. To rediscover the dialectic despite oneself is perhaps a more sure way of taking it seriously than by starting from it, by knowing the formula or schema in advance and applying it everywhere in virtue of one of those *general* convictions that Spinoza referred to knowledge of the first order, without asking how it comes about that being is dialectical. Pure perception would be the thing itself. But no perception is pure; every effective perception makes itself before a "center of indetermination" and distance, this being the price that must be paid for the "discernment" of an articulated perception. This is not an unconscious shift in Bergson, but is clearly worked out. He does not conceive nature simply as the fascinating object of perceptual experience, but rather as a horizon from which we are already far away, a primordial lost undividedness, a unity which the contradictions of the developed universe negate and express in their own way, and in this sense it is correct to view Bergson in a line with Schelling. The analysis of the *élan vital* resumes the problem of organic nature in the rigorous terms in which it was raised in the *Critique of Judgment*. Like Kant and Schelling, Bergson wanted to describe an operation or a natural production which proceeds from the whole to the parts, but owes nothing to the premeditation of the concept and admits of no teleological explanation. That is the reason why the description of life in the first chapters of *Creative Evolution* is scrupulously honest. At the same time it hides nothing of its blindness, its hesitations, and, on many points, its failures. Moreover, the fact that Bergson speaks of a "simple act," that he assigns reality to the *élan* in advance of its effects as a cause which contains them pre-eminently, contradicts his own concrete analyses, and it is in these that we should seek the remedy. Bergson finds his way back to philosophy with the help of Spencer, though not without groping. Once on his own path, he ended by rediscovering the problems of being, of the positive and the negative, the possible and the actual, in which following generations have been expert from the crib. Perhaps it is not such a bad way. At least he owes it to this method to have made upon these abstract—that is to say, difficult *et faciles*—topics some remarks which bear the value of true research. Leaving aside his polemics against the ideas of disorder, nothingness, and possibility, we have tried to disentangle a worthwhile meaning of Bergsonian "positivism," which could not be defended strictly, nor was ever held strictly by Bergson himself. There is in Bergson an organic possibility and negativity which are the ingredients of being. His precept of returning to the evidence of the real should not be understood as a naive apology for verification, but as an allusion to the pre-existence of natural being, always already there, which is the proper concern of the philosophy of nature.

We have in the end retraced the path (as it is to be found in *Ideen* II) by which Husserl, having himself started from the most rigorous imperative of reflection, returned to the problem of nature. At first sight, nature appears as the correlative of the sciences of nature, as a sphere of "pure things" (*blosse Sachen*) without any value predicate which is posited before a purely theoretical subject. The theme of such an "objective," scientific thought is part of our intentional apparatus and arises as soon as we try to seize, objectivate, get hold of or grasp the true which we immediately confound with the in-itself. Husserl does not set out to destroy this notion, but to comprehend, that is to say, to reveal the intentional life which sustains, grounds, and constitutes it, and is the measure of its truth. In one sense, he says, objective being envelops everything, even the activity of consciousness upon which we would like to make it rest. For the philosopher who constitutes objective being is a man, he has a body, that body is in nature, and thereby philosophies themselves have their time and place, occur in the *universum realitatis*. There is a truth in naturalism. But that truth is not naturalism itself. For to acknowledge naturalism and the envelopment of consciousness in the universe of *blosse Sachen* as an occurrence, is precisely to posit the theoretical world to which they belong as primary, which is an extreme form of idealism. It is in fact to refuse to decipher the intentional references which run from the universe of *blosse Sachen,* or extended objects, to "pretheoretical objects," to the life of consciousness before science. The *blosse Sachen* are the secondary expression, actively constructed by the pure subject, of the primordial stratum of intuitive, perceived things. The problem is to bring into the open the motivations which lead from the one to the other.

Now, the intuitive properties of the perceived object depend upon those of the "body-subject" (*Subjektleib*) who experiences them. Consciousness of my body as the organ of a motor power, of an "I can," is presupposed in the perception of two objects at a distance from each other or even in the identification of two successive perceptions which I have of the same object. Moreover, my body is a "field of localization" in which sensations are set up.

In the act of exploring objects my right hand touches my left hand, touches it touching, and in this encounters "a feeling thing." Since there is a body-subject and since it is before this that objects exist, they are virtually incorporated in my flesh. But at the same time, our body projects us into a world of convincing objects, we come to believe in "pure objects," establishing the attitude of pure knowledge and forgetting the density of the corporeal "preconstitution" which sustains them.

It is not adequate, however, to evoke the functioning of my body in isolation in order to account for the pure Cartesian "in-itself." For the object perceived in the tissue of my corporeal experience would still be far from being a pure or true object: it is caught in this bodily experience like in a cocoon; there is no discernment at all of what is true in it or of what is only appearance with respect to my particular experience of it. I am far from understanding them all, since my body, which is always primary, is not yet objectivated. This happens only when I think of my body as a body among all other human bodies, and, for example, imagine my eyes as typical of those eyes that I can see. The solipsistic object of perception can only become a pure object on the condition that my body enters into systematic relations with other animate bodies. The experience which I have of my body as a field of localization of an experience and that which I have of other bodies in so far as they *behave* in front of me, come before one another and pass into one another. There are two perceptions which illumine one another and are fulfilled together. On the one hand, there is the perception which I have of my body as the seat of a "vision," of a "touch," and (since the senses flow together in it to their source in the impalpable consciousness from which they arise) of the perception of an *I think*. On the other hand, there is the perception which I have deep down of another "excitable," "sensible" body which (since all that does not occur without an *I think*) is the bearer of another *I think*. Thus I cannot be quite the incomparable monster of solipsism that I see myself. I strip from my experience whatever is bound to my corporeal singularities. I am in face of an object which is truly an object for everyone. The *blosse Sachen* are possible, but as the correlative of an ideal community of embodied subjects, of an intercorporeality.

This genesis of a *Kosmotheoros* which remained schematic in *Ideen* II (and was in any case contradicted at every point by the thesis of the irrelativity of consciousness) is described again by Husserl in his later writings. He sketches the description of those pre-objective beings which are the correlates of a community of perceiving bodies and stakes out its primordial history. Beneath Cartesian nature, which theoretical activity sooner or later constructs, there emerges an anterior stratum, which is never suppressed, and which demands justification once the development of knowledge reveals the gaps in Cartesian science. Husserl risks the description of the earth as the seat of pre-objective spatiality and temporality, as the homeland and historicity of bodily subjects who are not yet disengaged observers, as the ground of truth or the ark which carries into the future the seeds of knowledge and culture. Before being manifest and "objective," truth dwells in the secret order of embodied subjects. At the root and in the depths of Cartesian nature there is another nature, the domain of an "originary presence" (*Ur-präsenz*) which, from the fact that it calls for the total response of a single embodied subject, is in principle present also to every other embodied subject.

Thus, a philosophy which seemed, more than any other, bent upon understanding natural being as the object and pure correlate of consciousness rediscovers through the very exercise of reflexive rigor a natural stratum in which the spirit is virtually buried in the concordant functioning of bodies within brute being. Cartesian nature had been conceived as self-sufficient, unable to lack being or not to be what it is, an inevitable being. At the end of the experience produced by this ontology European philosophy again confronts nature as an oriented and blind productivity. This does not represent a return to teleology. Properly speaking, teleology understood as the conformity of the event to a concept, shares the same fate as mechanism—these are both concepts of *artificialism*. Natural production has to be understood in some other way.

[2] CONTEMPORARY SCIENCE AND THE SIGNS OF A NEW CONCEPTION OF NATURE

In the last third of the year we began to look into contemporary science for the elements of a solution to the problem discussed above.

There is no need to justify the resort to science. Whatever one's conception of philosophy, its business is to elucidate experience, and science is a sector of our experience, admittedly subject to a very particular treatment by algorithm, yet in which in one way or another there is an encounter with being. This being so, it is not possible to reject science out of hand on the pretext that it works in terms of certain ontological prejudices. If these are indeed prejudices, then science itself, in its wanderings through being, will certainly have occasion to reject them. Being makes its path through science as through every individual life. From the interrogation of science philosophy stands to gain an encounter with certain articulations of being which otherwise it would find difficult to uncover.

Nevertheless one reservation must be made with regard to the philosophical use of scientific research: The philosopher, who lacks any professional competence in scientific techniques, should not pretend to intervene in the field, either in inductive research or to arbitrate for science. It is true that scientists' most general disputes do not arise over induction, as their most irreducible divergences show clearly enough. Here scientists try to express themselves at the level of language with the result that they cross over into philosophy. But this does not authorize philosophers to reserve to themselves the ultimate interpretation of scientific concepts. However, neither can they demand this interpretation from the scientists, who do not have it since they argue over it. Philosophers must find a way nicely between conceit and capitulation. This would involve asking science not what being is (science calculates *within being,* its constant procedure is to suppose the unknown known) but what being is certainly not; it would mean a scientific critique of the common notions outside of which philosophy cannot, on any hypothesis, establish itself. Science would contribute, as some physicists have said, "negative philosophical findings" (London and Bauer).

This is the spirit in which we have tried to show that science is always moving further away from the well-known definition of ontology given by Laplace. The critique of the classical concept of mechanics advanced in the past twenty-five years in wave mechanics could not possibly, whatever the outcome of the probabilistic interpretation, end in the restoration of Laplacean determinism. Here we have an intellectual experience which we have no right whatsoever to invoke in favor of a dogmatic acausality, but which alters the sense of causality. Even if one were, laboriously, to succeed by means of hidden parameters in putting its principles beyond reach—the very fact that they were hidden would reveal the occultism of dogmatic determinism. Certain philosophical descriptions of the perceived world may permit us to envisage what image of the world would positively express this self-criticism of determinism. For the perceived world is a world where there is discontinuity, where there is probability and generality, where each being is not constrained to a unique and fixed location, to an absolute density of being.

Similarly, the scientific critique of the forms of space and time in non-Euclidean geometry and relativity physics have taught us to break with the common notion of a space and time without reference to the observer's situation and enable us to give full ontological significance to certain descriptions of perceived space and time—to polymorphous space and time of which common sense and science retain only a few traces. Nor need the critique of absolute simultaneity in relativity physics necessarily lead to the paradoxes of the radical plurality of times—it might prepare the way for the recognition of a pre-objective temporality which is universal in its own way. Perceived time is, of course, solidary with the observer's point of view, but *by this fact* it constitutes the common dimension for all possible observers of one and the same nature. And this is so, not because we are constituted so as only to *attribute* to other observers an expanded or foreshortened time relative to our own—but rather the very contrary, in the sense that in its singularity our perceived time

announces to us other singularities and other perceived times, with the same rights as ours, and in
principle grounds the philosophical simultaneity of
a community of observers. In place of Laplace's
dogmatic objectivity, we glimpse an objectivity
pledged upon the inherence of all thinking subjects
in the same core of being which remains amorphous
but with whose presence they experiment from
within the situation to which they belong.

With all the more reason, a consideration of the
sciences which Auguste Comte and Cournot called
cosmological—that do not fix themselves upon constant relations but regard them as a means to recon-
structing the development of the world, and, for
example, of the solar system—would lead one to
establish a regression of eternal ideologies in which
nature is an object identical with itself and finally
the emergence of a history—or, as Whitehead said,
of a "process"—of nature. In the next course we
shall pursue this analysis in the field of the life
sciences.

9 / The Concept of Nature, II: Animality, the Human Body, Transition to Culture

IN ORDER TO SITUATE MORE CLEARLY the inquiry we are starting, we have decided to begin by going back to the relation between the problem of nature and the general problem of ontology. The study of nature is here an introduction to the definition of being, and in this respect one might just as well have started from man or God. In each case, it is a matter of knowing whether "being exists" is an analytic proposition, whether one can say quite simply that "being exists" and "nothingness does not exist." These questions, which could give rise to a whole philosophy, are raised in this instance from the standpoint of a certain sector of being, because it is perhaps a law of ontology always to proceed indirectly, and to lead up to being in general only through particular beings.

There are, for example, two senses of the word "nature" in Descartes (nature in the sense of "natu-

ral light" and nature in the sense of "natural inclination"). These two interpretations outline two ontologies (an ontology of the object and an ontology of
the existent) which Descartes attempted to reconcile in his later writings where he discovers the "being of God" (J. Laporte) beyond the possible and the
actual, beyond finality and causation, beyond will
and understanding in the "simple act," as E. Gil-
son and J. Laporte have both stressed. In Descartes as elsewhere, the notion of nature belongs to
an ontological complex, its avatars are the expression of a certain shift in the Cartesian ontology and
for this reason are of interest to us. It is possible
even that this shift in the Cartesian concept of nature is common to nearly all Western ontology. Can
we not find throughout our philosophy (and very
likely in our theology) a cycle or reverberation of a
thought which could be called "positivist" (being
exists, God exists by definition, if there has to be
some thing, it could only be this world and this
nature here, nothingness has no properties) and a
"negativist" thought (the first truth is that of a
doubt, what is certain first of all is a locus between
being and nothingness, the model of infinity is my
liberty, this world here is a pure fact) which inverts
the signs and perspectives of the former, without
either eliminating or coinciding with it? Do we not
find everywhere the double certitude that being exists, that appearances are only a manifestation and
a restriction of being—and that these appearances
are the canon of everything that we can understand

by "being," that in this respect it is being in-itself which appears as an ungraspable phantom, an *Un-ding*? Could we not find what has been called an "ontological diplopy" (Blondel), which after so much philosophical effort we cannot expect to bring to a rational reduction and which leaves us with the sole alternative of wholly embracing it, just as our gaze takes over monocular images to make a single vision out of them. Viewed in this way, the continual shifting of philosophies from one perspective to the other would not involve any contradiction, in the sense of inadvertence or incoherence, but would be justified and founded upon being. All one could do is to ask the philosopher to admit this phenomenon and to reflect upon it, rather than merely suffering it and occupying alternatively two ontological positions, each of which excludes and invites the other.

Perhaps then we would not regard the extraordinary confusion in modern ideas of nature, man, and God—the equivocations in "naturalism," "humanism," and "theism" (there is not one of these attitudes nowadays which does not slide into the other)—as nothing but decadence. If nowadays it happens that all the frontiers between these ideologies have broken down, this is because there is really, to borrow a phrase from Leibniz but in its strict sense, a "labyrinth of first philosophy." The task of philosophy should be to describe this labyrinth, to elaborate a concept of being such that its contradictions, neither accepted nor "transcended," still have their place. What was impossible for modern dialectical philosophies, because the dialectic which they contained remained bound by a predialectical ontology, would become possible in an ontology which reveals in being itself an overlap or movement.

We shall try here to arrive at this new ontology by following the recent development of the notion of nature. Applied science uncovers bodies of fact without ever achieving any radical self-expression, because it takes for granted traditional ontologies and never directly confronts the problem of being. But the transformations which it undergoes are full of philosophical significance. We shall attempt to develop these perspectives, to tie together the separate threads and to expose the "teleology" behind their progression.

We have gathered systematically last year's findings on the nature of physical being. At the very moment where twentieth-century physics has increased our power over nature to an unbelievable degree, it raises paradoxically the question of the meaning of its own truth in liberating itself from subjection to mechanical models and from figurative models in general. Physical action is no longer conceived as a trace in absolute space and time, passed on from one absolute individual to other equally absolute individuals. Physical entities, like mathematical entities, are no longer seen as "natures," but as "structures in an ensemble of operations." Determinism is no longer the tissue of the world: it is a crystallization on the surface of a "cloud" (Eddington). Some have remarked that this all reflects the return of "mentalism" in science. Others like Cassirer see in these developments a justification of critical idealism. On one point Cassirer is surely right: in the scientific description of the world there is no question of modern conceptions of causality implying an additional *factor* to be superimposed on the various determinisms. It is the latter which are always looked for, though what one discovers are only the supporting conditions outside of which the laws have no validity. What has occurred is a crisis in intuition rather than a crisis in science. For Cassirer, this crisis should make us understand once and for all what critical idealism had been teaching for a long time, namely, that symbolism does not have to be realized. Modern physics should disembarrass us not only of "materialism" and "mentalism," but of all philosophy of nature: nature is a "collection of relations which contain neither action nor passion." There can be no meaningful question concerning the *"Innere der Natur."* Nevertheless, this return to critical idealism does not take account of certain aspects of modern physics described by Cassirer himself. For there is a crisis, he says, not only of intuition, but of *Objektbegriff*. The field "is no longer a thing, it is a system of effects." But, if the concept of object is in dispute, how can critical idealism remain intact since it is entirely an analysis of the conditions and means of the positing of an object? Transcendental idealism loses its meaning if science has no power over the object.

What is called nature is certainly not a spirit at work in things whose aim is to resolve problems by "the most simple means"—but neither is it simply the projection of a power of thought or determination present in us. It is *that which makes there be,* simply, and at a single stroke such a coherent structure of a being, which we then laboriously express in speaking of a "space-time continuum," of "curved space," or simply of "the most determinate path" of the anaclastic line. Nature is that which establishes privileged states, the "dominant traits" (in the genetic sense of the word) which we try to comprehend through the combination of concepts—nature is an ontological derivation, a pure "passage," which is neither the only nor the best one possible, which stands at the horizon of our thought as a fact which there can be no question of deducing.

This facticity of nature is revealed to us in the universe of perception. Whatever the corrections which knowledge has to make in it, this universe regains an ontological signification that it had lost in classical science. As Niels Bohr has remarked, it is no accident that there is a harmony between the descriptions of psychology (we would say, of phenomenology) and the conceptions of contemporary physics. Moreover, the classical criticism of the perceived universe is bound to a mechanistic psychophysiology which can no longer be retained as such at a time when scientists are throwing doubt upon mechanistic metaphysics.

In the last half of the year we tried, in the same way, to specify the concept of organic nature implicit in contemporary science. The life sciences also never cease to introduce "operational" concepts whose obscurity should not be dissipated but circumscribed and reflected upon philosophically. There are, for example, the concepts of behavior (in the sense of Coghill and Gesell) and those of information and communication which, throughout all the discussion to which they give rise, elude the classical interpretations they were intended to rejoin. We attempted to analyze the notions of the possible, of totality, form, field, and signification around which these investigations gravitate.

Unlike that of physics, the development of the contemporary life-sciences does not occur in the form of extensive theoretical unifications. Thus instead of a connected account we can provide only samples and selections. Several lectures were devoted to the different levels of behavior.

Lower-order behavior was examined in terms of the perspective offered by J. von Uexüll and the notions of *Umwelt, Merkwelt* and *Wirkwelt* which he has introduced. We discussed the notion of *Subjektnatur* which he believed to be the conclusion of his findings. We traced the application of the concept of behavior in morphogenesis and physiology ("behavior in internal circuits," for example in E. S.

Russell).[1] This introduced the ideas of a thematization, in opposition to a "pushed-causality," and of a "directiveness," although limited and specialized and to that extent as different from the notion of entelechy as from the notion of machine. The forms of lower-order behavior also introduced us to a mutual cohesion between the parts of the organism, the organism and its surroundings, between organisms and the species, which involves a sort of presignification.

Reciprocally, we should find among the so-called higher levels of behavior (the study of which, by Lorenz for example, derives directly from Uexüll) something of the inertia of the body. If animal being is already a production (*faire*) then there is an activity of the animal which is not simply an extension of its being. In mimesis, where it is impossible to separate behavior and morphology, there appears a fundamental level of behavior where resemblance is operative, a "natural magic," or a vital undividedness, which involves neither finality nor a relation of understanding and representation. Portmann's idea of a reading of animal types (*Tiergestalt*), a study of their external appearance considered as an "organ for being seen," with its accompanying notion of an interanimality as necessary to the complete definition of the organism as its hormones and its "internal" processes, has offered further verifica-

1. E. S. Russell, *The Directiveness of Organic Activities* (Cambridge: At the University Press, 1945).—*Trans.*

tion of the theme of the organism's "form value." It is in terms of these notions that we opened up the study of "instinctive movements" of "sign stimuli," and of "innate activating schemas" referred to by Lorenz, trying to show that these do not imply any renewal of mechanism, suggested by the metaphors of lock and key, but of spontaneous styles of behavior which anticipate an aspect or element of the world and are occasionally sufficiently open to give rise to a fixation on a nonspecific element (*Prägung*). Thus, since the instinct is an oneiric or narcissistic preparation of external "objects," it is not surprising that it is capable of substitutions, displacements, of "action at a distance," and of "ritualizations" which do not merely superimpose themselves upon fundamental biological acts, such as copulation, but displace them, transfigure them, and submit them to conditions of "display" which reveal the appearance of a being who *sees* and *shows himself*, with the emergence of a symbolism whose "comparative philology" (Lorenz) [2] has yet to be constructed.

We also tried to get at the nature of vital being by following the method of epistemology, that is to say, through reflection upon the knowledge of living creatures. We inquired into the conditions under which we may validly attribute to a given animal one or more "senses," an associated milieu or "territory," a working relation with its cohort (Chauvin's

2. Konrad Lorenz, "Über tanzähnliche Bewegungsweisen bei Tieren," *Studium Generale*, V, no. 1 (1952).—*Trans.*

study of the migratory locust) and finally a symbolic life (Frisch's study of language in bees). It
emerged that all zoology assumes from our side a
methodical *Einfühlung* into animal behavior, with
the participation of the animal in our perceptive life
and the participation of our perceptive life in ani-
mality. In such phenomena we have found a new
argument against the philosophical artificialism of
neo-Darwinism in its most developed forms. The
ultra-mechanism or ultra-finalism of the Darwini-
ans rests upon the ontological principle of all or
nothing: an organism *is* absolutely what it is; if it
were not, it would have been deprived of existence
by the given conditions. The result of this way of
thinking is to mask the most remarkable characteristic of living homeostases, namely, invariance
through fluctuation. Whether we are dealing with
organisms or animal societies, we do not find things
subject to a law of all or nothing, but rather dynamic, unstable equilibria in which every rearrange-
ment resumes already latent activities and trans-
figures them by decentering them. As a result, one
cannot conceive of the relations between species or
between the species and man in terms of a hierarchy. What there is is a difference of quality and
for this very reason living creatures are not superimposed upon one another, the transcendence of
one by the other is, so to speak, lateral rather than
frontal, and one meets all sorts of anticipations and
reminiscences.

In order to make contact with indubitably organic facts, we came back to ontogenesis and to embryology in particular—and showed that mechanistic interpretations (Speeman) as well as those of Driesch lose what is essential in the new notion of the possible: namely, the possible conceived not as another eventual occurrence, but as an ingredient of the existing world itself, as *general reality*.

In terms of this preview, which we shall complete at the beginning of next year by sketching the problems of the systematic theory of descent, we may already say that the ontology of life, as well as that of "physical nature," can only escape its troubles by resorting, apart from all artificialism, to brute being as revealed to us in our perceptual contact with the world. It is only within the perceived world that we can understand that all corporeality is already symbolism. Next year we shall attempt to describe in more detail the emergence of symbolism in the transition to the level of the human body.[3]

3. "Symbolism and the Human Body"; see translator's note on p. 99.

10 / Philosophy as Interrogation[1]

WITH THE PERMISSION of the Minister of Education to abridge the course, we have decided to postpone until next year the continuation of the study we began on the ontology of nature,[2] and to devote this year to some general reflections on the meaning of this inquiry and the question of the possibility of philosophy today.

What exactly are we looking for when we try to abstract from nature the categories of substance, accident, potentiality, act, object, subject, in-itself, for-itself, which are traditionally involved in ontology? What can be the relation between the new

1. This course was announced as "Symbolism and the Human Body." We venture to redescribe it since, as is clear from the opening remarks, it is concerned with the question of the possibility of philosophy today.—*Trans.*

2. Permission to abridge the course was granted in order to give Merleau-Ponty more time to work on the manuscript of *The Visible and the Invisible*.—*Trans.*

ontology and classical metaphysics? Could it be the negation and the end of philosophy, or, on the contrary, is it perhaps the very same inquiry restored to its vital sources?

With Hegel something comes to an end. After Hegel, there is a philosophical void. This is not to say that there has been a lack of thinkers or of geniuses, but that Marx, Kierkegaard, and Nietzsche start from a denial of philosophy. We might say that with the latter we enter an age of non-philosophy. But perhaps such a destruction of philosophy constitutes its very realization. Perhaps it preserves the essence of philosophy, and it may be, as Husserl wrote,[3] that philosophy is reborn from its ashes.

We shall not find the answer to these questions by following the history of thought since Hegel. The great works to be found along this path are too preoccupied with the struggle against Hegel and classical metaphysics, and to this extent have too much in common with them, to permit us to see clearly what remains of philosophy in these non-philosophies. On this point their obscurities and equivocations are beyond repair. The interpretations which they offer, and which we believe enable us to ascertain their content, actually only reflect our own views and problems. Nowadays, any commentary

3. *Die Krisis der europäischen Wissenschaften und die transzendentale Phänomenologie,* ed. Walter Biemel, *Husserliana* VI (The Hague: Martinus Nijhoff, 1962) [English translation, *The Crisis of European Sciences and Transcendental Phenomenology,* by David Carr (Evanston, Ill.: Northwestern University Press, 1970)].

on Marx or even Nietzsche is actually only a dis-
guised stand with regard to our own times. Through
a turn of events which itself is legitimate, those
writers who refused the title of philosophers and
deliberately devoted themselves to deciphering their
own times—even though they may provide a language for their successors, an interrogation, the beginnings of analyses with a quite new depth—cannot by contrast *guide* posterity: it is to posterity
itself that they leave the task of giving the final
meaning to their work. They live on in us rather
than our having a clear perspective on them and we
involve them in our own problems rather than solv-
ing theirs with ours.

Everything occurs as though these philosophers
had anticipated a world which turns out to be our
own, as though the world had made an effort to
resemble what they had foretold. For once, thought
was in advance of history, and the questions they
raised illuminate the present in which we live. By
contrast, their answers, the solutions which they
offer to that history which they anticipated so well
—whether it is Marx's praxis or Nietzsche's will to
power—seem to us too simple. They were conceived
in opposition to metaphysics yet within the shelter
of the solid world of which metaphysics is a part.
For us who have to deal with the bewitched world
foreseen by Marx and Nietzsche their solutions are
inadequate to the nature of the crisis. In place of a
philosophy which—at least in principle and *ex offi-
cio*—stood for clarity against possibly different re-

plies to the same problems, we see more and more a history of non-philosophy whose authors have as their sole common denominator a certain modern obscurity, a pure interrogation. We shall not find the new philosophy already developed in Marx or in Nietzsche. We have to create it, taking into account the world in which we live where it becomes clear that their negation of metaphysics cannot take the place of philosophy.

That is why, before examining two contemporary efforts, we wished to describe (without any pretense of being complete) some of the phenomena which, whether it be in the order of history or that of culture, discredit philosophy among us, perhaps eventually to bring it back to life.

With regard to the relations between men, even those thinkers who found no natural harmonies in this area did not, prior to our times, believe that society was condemned to chaos. Marx only described social relations as contradictory within the framework of a specific historical regime whose successor was marked out from the very start and his solution to the contradictions of history through history itself was universal, valid equally for nondeveloped as well as industrial societies. This core of universality around which history was to organize itself has disintegrated. It may properly be asked whether violence, the opacity of social relations and the difficulties of a world in which such questions are the order of the day and where such doubts are unavoidable (even to those in it who post up complete certitudes) secretes of itself a violence and a desperate counterviolence. History has exhausted the categories in which conservative thought confined it, and it has done the same with those of revolutionary thought. But it is not just that the human world is illegible, nature itself has become explosive. Technology and science range before us energies which are no longer *within* the framework of the world but are capable of destroying it. They provide us with means of exploration which, even before having been used, awaken the old desire and the old fear of meeting the absolute Other. What for centuries had, in the eyes of men, possessed the solidity of the earth now appears fragile; what was once our predestined horizon has now become a provisional perspective. But equally, since it is man who discovers and fabricates, a new prometheism is mixed with our experience of the prehuman world. An extreme naturalism and an extreme artificialism are inextricably associated, not only in the myths of everyday life, but also in the refined myths which arise, for example, out of the theory of information or neo-Darwinism.

Considering these facts alone, the balance of our experience would seem to be negative. But, in the order of culture and research, the relativization of what was believed to be the ground of history and of nature is already found to possess a new solidity. Whether one thinks of the rejection of a ready-made language, meaningful from the very start, which has occurred from Mallarmé to the surrealists, or of the rejection of "means of representation" and of the systems of equivalences constituted in modern painting, or, again, of the generalization of music beyond the traditional selections in tonal and instrumental music, the very understanding of the classical forms of art has been renewed by the transcendence of counterpoint systems and the search for nonfigurative invariants. In all these domains, as well as in psychoanalysis, considered as a social and almost popular phenomenon, disintegration has found a balance and is surpassed, in the case of the better practitioners, by a new sense of the plurality of possibilities; the menace of the technical spirit has been offset by the expectation of a free reintegration.

Among philosophers the positive aspect of experience is decidedly the dominant one. Driven to self-examination by the irrationalism of their times, as well as by the intrinsic evolution of their problems, philosophers have arrived at a definition of philosophy as the interrogation of its very own meaning and possibility. "What I seek under the name of philosophy," writes Husserl,[4] "as the goal and the field of my labor, I know naturally. And yet I do not know it. Has this 'knowledge' ever been sufficient for any true thinker (*Selbstdenker*)? Has "philosophy ever ceased to be a riddle to him in his life as a philosopher?"—But this problem, this astonishment before one's self, and the unhabituated and unhabit-

4. *Ibid.*, Appendix 28, Supplementary Text, pp. 508–13.

ual vision which is its result, are precisely philosophy, are "what, in the last analysis, *was intended* in the hidden unity of intentional interiority, which alone creates the unity of history." [5]

We have attempted to retrace the path by which Husserl passed from "philosophy as a strict science" to philosophy as pure interrogation—the same path which led Heidegger to the negativist and anthropological themes to which the public reduced his early writings, to a conception of Being which he no longer calls philosophy—but which, as it has been well remarked (J. Beaufret), is certainly not extra-philosophical.

In Husserl it is clear that the pure interrogation is not a residue from metaphysics, not its last breath nor a yearning for its lost empire. It is the proper means of opening us to the world, to time, to nature, to contemporary and living history and a means of accomplishing the perpetual ambitions of philosophy. For if anyone ever engaged in those ambitions, it was indeed Husserl. He undertook them wholly and naively at the beginning of the century when he made philosophy an inventory of the "essences" which, in every domain of experience, resist our efforts at an imaginative variation and are thus the invariants of the domain in question. But, even at this time, he dealt with essences as they are experienced by us, as they emerge from our intentional life. This is what Husserl should have expressed, in

5. *Ibid.*, p. 74.

the middle period of his thought, in the doctrine of the "reduction" as a return to the immanent meaning of our experiences, and in the formula of "phenomenological idealism." However, the process of reduction needs to be scrutinized and clarified. It then appears to involve a paradox. In one sense, what it teaches us is already known to us in the natural attitude, through the "world thesis." But Husserl's analysis elucidates the bodily infrastructure of our relation with things and with others, and it appears difficult to "constitute" these brute materials out of the attitudes and operations of consciousness which derives from a different order, that of theoria and ideation. The method of reduction is jeopardized by this internal difficulty in the "constitutive phenomenology." It is similarly at issue through certain of its implications, which were at first unnoticed but caught Husserl's attention in the period of the *Cartesian Meditations* (1929) and when developed revealed the reduction as less of a method defined once and for all than the index of a multitude of problems. The philosopher who advocates the reduction speaks for everyone; he implies that what is evident for him is or could be for everyone; he therefore implies an intersubjective universe and remains, relative to that universe, in the attitude of naive faith. An integral philosophy ought to be able to explicate and to constitute that domain. But how can I give an account of my access to *the alter ego*—even if he were reduced to the "meaning" *alter*

ego—as the immanent operation of my consciousness? This would be tantamount to constituting the
other person as constituting, and, through him, to
reduce myself to the status of the one constituted.
Furthermore, with regard to what concerns the
other person, can I, or can he, with regard to what
concerns me, make the distinction which I make
between myself as the ultimate, constituting subject
and the empirical man in whom this constituting
subject is embodied—a distinction which I make
easily through reflection and by a secondary apper-
ception of which I am still the author? To an external observer, is not the ultimate and constituting
subject one and the same as existent with the empirical man? Is not Fichte's *Ichheit überhaupt* simply
Fichte? The *Cartesian Meditations* grasp both horns
of the dilemma: there is an indeclinable subjectivity, an insurmountable solipsism—and yet, for this
very subjectivity, there is an intentional "transgres-
sion" or "encroachment" which enables everything
which happens within itself to pass into the other
person.

It is in the last work which Husserl himself
prepared for publication that the difficulties in the
phenomenological reduction make themselves felt
to the point where they broach upon a fresh mutation in the doctrine of the reduction. From then on
Husserl describes the reduction as an initial phase
of inquiry, characteristic of phenomenology—perhaps even coextensive with phenomenology. It is a

question here, he says, of a type of being which contains everything: *allumspannende Seinsweise* [6] —the return from an objective world to a *Lebenswelt* in whose continual flux are borne Nature and the objects of perception, as well as the constructions through which we grasp them with Cartesian exactness; it is the source in general of all the historical structures which help us to analyze or model our relations with others and with the truth. When translated in terms of the *Lebenswelt*, the antinomies in the constitution of *alter* or those in the world thesis cease to be hopeless. We no longer have to try to understand how a for-itself can think of another from the ground of its own absolute solitude or how it could think of a preconstituted world in the very moment that it constitutes the world: the inherence of the self-in-the-world or of the world-in-the-self, what Husserl calls the *Ineinander*, is silently inscribed in an all-embracing experience which composes these incompossibles, and philosophy becomes the enterprise of describing, outside of the logic and vocabulary at hand, the universe of living paradoxes. The reduction no longer involves a return to ideal being, but brings us back to the spirit of Heraclitus,[7] to an interweaving of horizons, to an open Being. Through having "forgotten" the flux of the natural and historical world, having reduced it to the constructions of the objectivity of the natural sciences, reason and philosophy have become incap-

6. *Ibid.*, p. 134.
7. *Ibid.*, p. 173.

able of understanding and so of mastering man's historical fate. The horizon of "infinite tasks" opened up in the sixteenth and seventeenth centuries has dropped out of sight, while reason and philosophy have compromised with an ideal of objectivism which made knowledge of the mind and history an impossibility.

Heidegger's path, no less than Husserl's, is difficult to trace, and for the same reasons—namely, that commentators have fixed upon what recalled for them philosophy's past. Hardly any have followed the authors in what was nevertheless their main effort: to recover through an absolutely new way of thinking the experience which underlies metaphysics. In the early works of Heidegger, the emphasis has been put upon the role of the concept of Nothingness and the definition of a man as the locus of Nothingness. That is why some have looked in Heidegger for the substitution of humanism in place of metaphysics, and, whether they have been happy to find metaphysics destroyed or have made use of it in order to restore it, they have misconstrued his views on the human situation as he described it. In both cases, commentators have missed what, from the Preface to *Sein und Zeit*, was the declared aim of his thought: not to describe existence, *Dasein* (which has been incorrectly translated in French as "human reality"), as a fundamental and autonomous sphere—but, through *Da-sein*, to get at Being, the analysis of certain human attitudes being undertaken only because man *is* the interrogation of Being. Soon after *Sein und Zeit,* the analysis of truth and our openness to truth took the all too well-known path of the descriptions of anxiety, freedom, and concern. Heidegger speaks less and less of the relation of *ekstasis* between us and being, which underlies the priority of the self and the centrifugal movement of the self toward being. He dissolves the equivocations by pointing out that for him there was never any question of reducing being to time, but of approaching being through time, that in an absolute sense Nothingness (the Nothing nihilates, the *nichtiges Nichts*) cannot be taken into consideration. Existence, in contrast to Beings, or the things that are there in the world, can, if one wishes, be treated as non-being, but that is not nothing or nihilation. It is beyond such correlatives—the object and the Nothing "nihilates"—that philosophy takes its start, namely, in a "there exists," in an "opening" toward "something," toward "that which is not nothing." It is this preobjective Being, between the inert essence or *quidditas* and the individual localized at a point of space-time, that is the proper theme of philosophy. It can be said of this Being—the rose, said Angelus Silesius, is "without any why," blooms because it blooms, the rose-spectacle, the rose-totality—that it has no cause outside of itself, and moreover is not the cause of itself, that it is without ground, being the absence in principle of any ground. What more can be said of this radiation of qualified being, of this active being, or action of "standing-in" as one translator has put it? Unlike other words, the word to be is not a sign to which one could find a corresponding "representation" or object: its meaning is not distinct from its operation, which is to make Being speak in us rather than us speak of Being. For how would we speak of Being, since those beings and shapes of Being, which open to us the only conceivable access to it, at the same time hide it from us by their mass, and since every unveiling is simultaneously a dissimulation? What has been called the "mystique" of Being —a word expressly rejected by Heidegger—is the effort to integrate truth with our capacity for error, to relate the incontestable presence of the world to its inexhaustible richness and consequent absence which it recuperates, to consider the evidence of Being in the light of an interrogation which is the only mode of expressing this eternal elusion. We have tried to show how a philosophy oriented in this way leads us to a complete reworking of the concepts ordinarily used in the analysis of language (such as those of sign, meaning, analogon, metaphor, symbol) and how it leads to the notion of an "ontological history" (*Seinsgeschichte*) which stands to an empirical history of human actions and passions as a philosophical apprehension of speaking stands to the analysis of linguistic materials.

If we call philosophy the quest of Being or the *Ineinander*, is not philosophy quickly brought to silence—that very silence which from time to time breaks into Heidegger's essays? But does not this come from Heidegger's search for a direct expression of what is fundamental at the very moment he is showing its impossibility? Is it not the result of his refusal of all the mirrors of Being? It is the aim of an inquiry such as we have pursued here on the ontology of nature to sustain through contact with existents and the exploration of the regions of Being the same attention to what is fundamental that remains the privilege and the task of philosophy.

11 / Husserl at the Limits of Phenomenology

SINCE WE STILL LACK a complete edition of Husserl's *Nachlass*, the following discussion can hardly pretend to be "objective" in the sense of saying just what was said or directly implied by Husserl in the whole context of his writings. But even when everything of Husserl is published, are we right to assume that the "objective" method would restore to us "the thought" of Husserl? Such an assumption would only be plausible if Husserl's thought, or that of any other philosopher, were simply a system of neatly defined concepts, arguments to perennial questions and replies in which problems are permanently solved. But what if the act of reflection changes the meaning of the concepts it employs and perhaps even the nature of its questions; what if its conclusions are merely the overall direction of a search which was transformed into a "work" by the ever premature interruption of a life's work? Then we could not define a philosopher's thought solely in terms of what he had achieved. We should have to take account of what until the very end he was struggling to bring to reflection. Naturally, this unfinished thought (*impensé*) must be shown to be present through the words which circumscribe and delimit it. But then these words must be understood through their lateral implications as much as through their manifest or frontal significance. We need what Husserl called a "poetry of the history of philosophy" that would give us access to an operant thought, which in the case of a contemporary thinker would not be so risky, and perhaps be the only mode of objectivity in treating one who has written: *"Das historisch an sich Erste ist unsere Gegenwart."* [1]

While only a complete edition can validate our interpretation, although hardly ever dispense with it, why not start right now to study the texts? In view of the rumors and discussion which always arise around a posthumous doctrine, such a start is imperative. For there are some who fear or wish to see Husserl "deviate" into the path of irrationalism that they believe Heidegger took. The best approach to this problem is to study the texts, two of them in particular.

The first text to be considered is "Die Frage nach dem Ursprung der Geometrie als intentional-histo-

---

1. "Our present is intrinsically historical."—*Trans.*

risches Problem." [2] It is because ideality and histo-ricity have a common source that it is not by chance that there is an unfinished history of geometry which remains open, while at the same time there is a corpus of geometry which forms a system (*Total-sinn*) in which the early steps seem to have been cancelled insofar as they were partial or contingent developments.

To discover that common source, one has only to locate between the flow of events and the timeless realm of meaning a third dimension, which would be a subterranean history or the genesis of ideality. Both the early stages of geometry as well as all its later advances contain a certain surplus of meaning over and beyond their manifest or literal sense as it enters the experience of individual geometricians. Each stage opens up a field and prepares themes which their author can only see as an outline of what is to come (*Urstiftung*), but which, when *handed down* (*tradiert*) to succeeding generations along with the earliest advances, become useful through a sort of second creation (*Nachstiftung*). In this process new dimensions of thought are opened up until, once the development has run its course and has ended up in a last re-creation (*End-stiftung*), there intervenes a mutation in knowl-

2. *Die Krisis der europäischen Wissenschaften und die transzendentale Phänomenologie,* ed. Walter Biemel, *Hus-serliana* VI (The Hague: Martinus Nijhoff, 1962), pp. 365–86 [English translation, *The Crisis of European Sciences and Transcendental Phenomenology,* by David Carr (Evanston, Ill.: Northwestern University Press, 1970)].

edge, often the result of a return to the sources or the side-paths neglected by the mainstream, which results in a new interpretation of all that went before. The historical development or the *Beweglichkeit* of geometry only coincides with its ideal sense for the reason that the latter is the perception of a field, a beginning or an opening which requires an endless production and reproduction. The principal role of every idea, once it has been formulated, signed, and dated, is to make its literal repetition superfluous, to launch culture toward a future, to achieve oblivion, to be transcended, to outline the horizon of a geometry to come and to delimit a coherent domain. In turn, it is essential for any system of ideas to be born, and to yield to us only in the furrow of historicity. Even if we knew nothing about the originators of geometry, we would at least know that there had been such individuals; geometry is never a natural phenomenon like the stones and the mountains. It exists only in the "space of humanity"; it belongs to being which has become spiritual (*geistig geworden*) and will continue to do so. Spiritual being exists solely for a mind resolved to reflect actively, determined to go on, to plunge itself still further into the invisible realm of unreal creations. Ideality coincides with historicity because it rests upon acts and because "the only way to grasp an idea is to produce it." The idea is impalpable and invisible because it has been *made.* The historicity of an idea is not the fact of its inclusion in a series of events with a unique temporal location, or its origin in the mind of a particular man living at a certain place and time. It is its function to situate a task which is not uniquely its own, but one that echoes back to earlier beginnings. The historicity of an idea summons up the whole past and the entire future of culture as its witness. And to call upon so much history it has no need of documents, for history has its anchorage within itself, in the flesh of its sensible or natural existence, its active and productive being. It has only to reflect in order to know that thought makes itself, that it is culture and history.

How are we to understand this reverberation of the past and this pre-possession (*Vorhaben*) of the future of thought in any contemporary thought? In one sense geometry or any particular truth of geometry exists once for all, no matter how often it is thought of by individual geometricians. But if there was a pure and detached ideality, how would it enter the consciousness of he who discovers it, how would it come to birth in anyone's mind? Yet, on the other hand, if we start, as we must, from its birth in us, how shall we get from there to an ideal being, beyond any existing or possible mind? The only answer is that we do so by referring back to the implications of experience. A signification leaves its "place in consciousness" when it has been *said*. It is in virtue of being *Sinn von Reden* that it is there "for everyone," for every real or possible interlocutor. But language is "interwoven" (*verflochten*) with our horizon upon the world and humanity. Language is borne by our relation to the world and to others, which in turn supports and creates it. It is through language that our horizon is open and endless (*endlos*) and it is because we know that "everything has a name" that each thing exists and has a way of existing for us. To exist for us geometry inherits this linguistic tradition. But language only makes a signification universally available when it makes the objects of the world "public." Hence geometry is not merely an appropriation of a particular living mind, even though everyone agrees on such an ascription. Thus we have still not given a complete account of ideal being.

Neither have we exhausted the powers of "speech." Before anything else within my sphere of consciousness there is a sort of message from myself to myself: I can be sure today of thinking the same thought that I thought yesterday because the wake which it leaves is or could be retraced exactly by a fresh act of productive thought, which is the only veritable fulfillment of my recollected thought. I think in this near past, or rather yesterday's thought passes into today's thought: there is an encroachment of the passive upon the active which is reciprocal. Speech passes from the sphere of one consciousness to another by the same phenomenon of encroachment or propagation. As a speaking and active subject I encroach upon the other who is listening, as the understanding and passive subject I allow the other to encroach upon me. Within myself and in the exercise of language I experience activity in every case as the other side of passivity. And it is thus that ideality "makes its entrance" (*Eintritt*). No more in my relationship to myself than in my relationship to others is there any question of survey or of pure ideality. There is, however, the recuperation of a passivity by an activity: that is how I think within the other person and how I talk with myself. Speech is not a product of my active thought, standing in a secondary relation to it. It is my practice, my way of working, my *"Funktion,"* my destiny. Every production of the spirit is a response and an appeal, a coproduction.

But ideal being subsists outside of all actual communication, when the speaking subjects are asleep or are no longer living, and it seems to pre-exist speech, since there are men yet to be born who later will form valid ideas and these ideas are no less valid at this present moment. However, this does not place ideal being outside of speech, but merely obliges us to introduce an essential mutation in speech, namely, the appearance of writing. It is writing which once and for all translates the meaning of spoken words into ideal being, at the same time transforming human sociability, inasmuch as writing is "virtual" communication, the speaking of *x* to *x*, which is not carried by any living subject and belongs in principle to everyone, evoking a total speech. But the pure meaning contained in the written page which sublimates the solidity of things and then communicates that sublimation to thought is also a petrified meaning, sedimented, latent or dormant, insofar as no living spirit comes along to arouse it. The moment one touches the total meaning, one touches upon absence and the forgotten as well. Living meaning extends far beyond our explicit thoughts, but it is only open and without an end; it is not infinite. The sedimentation which makes it possible for us to go further is also responsible for us being threatened by hollow thoughts and for the sense of origins becoming void. The true cannot be defined outside of the possibility of the false.

We have now reached Husserl's last meditations on my relation to myself and to others, of which we can get a glance, while waiting for the publication of the manuscripts, from a fine study by Eugen Fink.[3] Passivity and activity, the spontaneous "I" and sensible time, cannot remain mutually external since I function as thinker identical through time and intersubjectivity is also in play. There is thus a sort of "simultaneity" of the one and the other, an *Urgegenwart* which has no locus between the before and after, an *Ur-Ich* anterior to the plurality of monads which cannot be said to be singular either, because it precedes both unity and plurality—true "negativity," "diremption," a being prior to the distinction between essence and existence. These words, says Fink, project the new dimension of *Le-*

3. "Die Spätphilosophie Husserls in der Freiburger Zeit," in *Edmund Husserl, 1859–1959, Phaenomenologica* IV (The Hague: Martinus Nijhoff, 1960), pp. 99–115.

benstiefe which opens up in the writings of Husserl's later period. But for Husserl this speculative vocabulary was only an aid to description, a means of outlining the operation of the transcendental life which he always sought to catch in the act, analytically. His philosophy is not congealed in "results," or "points of view." Moreover, Husserl's later philosophy is no finished product, no fixed possession of the cultural spirit, no house in which one can dwell comfortably. "Everything is open, all its paths lead out into the open." [4] To come back to the problem of ideality, Husserl's analyses foreshadow Heidegger's thoughts on the way speech speaks.[5]

The notions of openness and horizon, employed in the fragment on the origin of geometry with regard to superstructures and ideal being, are to be found also with regard to the "base" in a text from 1934, *Umsturz der kopernikanischen Lehre*.[6] For the Copernican, the world contains only "bodies" (*Körper*). Through meditation we must again learn of a mode of being whose conception we have lost, the being of the "ground" (*Boden*), and that of the earth first of all—the earth where we live, that which is this side of rest and movement, being the ground from which all rest and all movement are

4. *Ibid.*, pp. 113–14.
5. *Unterwegs zur Sprache* (Pfullingen: Neske, 1958), pp. 12–13.
6. Unpublished. We have this from communication in 1939 with Professor Aron Gurwitsch, one of Husserl's students.

separated, which is not made out of *Körper,* being the "source" from which they are drawn through division, which has no "place," being that which surrounds all place, which lifts all particular beings out of nothingness, as Noah's Ark preserved the living creatures from the Flood. There is a kinship between the being of the earth and that of my body (*Leib*) which it would not be exact for me to speak of as moving since my body is always at the same distance from me. This kinship extends to others, who appear to me as other bodies, to animals whom I understand as variants of my embodiment, and finally even to terrestrial bodies since I introduce them into the society of living bodies when saying, for example, that a stone "flies." To the degree that I adopt the Copernican constitution of the world, I abandon my own standpoint, I pretend to be an absolute observer, forgetting my terrestrial roots which nevertheless nourish everything else, and I come to consider the world as the pure object of an infinite reflection before which there are only objects conformable to itself. But such an idealization cannot provide its own foundation, and the sciences of the infinite are experiencing a crisis. The type of being which our experience of the earth and the body reveals to us is no curiosity of external perception but has a philosophical signification. Our implantation envelops a view of space and temporality, a view of natural causation, of our "territory." It envelops an *Urhistorie* which binds all existing or possible societies insofar as they all inhabit the same "earthly" space, in the broadest sense, and finally it contains a philosophy of the world as *Offenheit der Umwelt,* in opposition to the "represented" infinite of the classical sciences of nature.

12 / Nature and Logos: The Human Body

FIRST OF ALL, we have completed our analysis from earlier years of certain examples of biological thought relative to the organic development of the organism, and the problems of ontogenesis and phylogenesis. It seemed to be of interest to follow the detours in Driesch's thinking inasmuch as contemporary embryology is still preoccupied with the same questions raised by Driesch over sixty years ago. Driesch maintained that the organism cannot be reduced to its state at any given moment, since the activities of regulation and regeneration are indications of an excess of the potential over the actual. At the same time, Driesch was reluctant to label these potentialities "prospective powers," since it would be necessary to add a principle of order which guaranteed the invariance of the type, and since in combination these two principles would obviously only be an "analytic" expression of what took place. Occasionally, however, Driesch regards development as a network of reciprocal actions in which the "directive stimuli" interact with one another, which would leave the factor E (entelechy) with nothing more than a symbolic value. Nevertheless, Driesch is not free from the alternatives of the machine or life: if the organism is not a machine, then entelechy must be "the expression of a true reality, of a veritable element of nature," and since this reality is invisible to science, there must be a "thought" or philosophy which takes the place of science to determine this second positivity indirectly designated by science. Here what is instructive is that, while making the transition to "philosophy," Driesch, who is an exacting thinker, feels constrained to deny entelechy the status of energy, transformer of energy, or even "releaser," recognizing in it only the power to suspend suspensions or equilibria, and finally delimiting it as simply "a complicated system of negations." [1] One could only go further, he says, by departing from the experience of "my body" and its relation with space—a path familiar to our contemporaries, but which only leads back to the same problems if "my body" is only an island in a mechanical world. In our opinion, the difficulties which Driesch encountered show that life is incomprehensible both to the philosophy of the object (mechanism *and* vitalism) and to the philosophy of the idea, and can only be clarified

1. A. E. Driesch, *The Science and Philosophy of the Organism* (London: A. and C. Black, 1929).—*Trans.*

through a philosophy of "something," or, as one says nowadays, a philosophy of structure. Embryology since Driesch seems to us to have been moving in this direction in refusing to opt either for preformation or epigenesis, rather taking both notions as "complementary" and describing embryogenesis as a "flux of determination." The appearance of the notions of "gradient" and "fields"—that is to say, of "organo-formative" territories which impinge upon one another and possess a periphery beyond their focal region in which regulation is only probable— represents a mutation in biological thought as important as anything in physics. Physicists are rejecting both the restriction of space and the resort to a second positive causality; they conceive life as a sort of reinvestment of physical space, the emergence of original macrophenomena between the microphenomena, "singular areas" of space or "enveloped phenomena."

The need for new theoretical frameworks is also felt in the study of phylogenesis. The neo-Darwinists had attempted to frame their descriptions of the "style" or "design" of evolution (micro-evolution, macro-evolution, mega-evolution) in the schema of selection-mutation inherited from Darwin. But they managed to do so only by weighting their schema with a quite new sense, so that in a recent work Simpson writes: "The cause of an evolutionary event is the *total* situation preceding it . . . so that it is not entirely realistic to attempt designation of separate causal elements within that situation. At most, one may speak of 'factor complexes' or 'constellations.' " [2] From this point of view, there is no longer any place for argument over the predominance of mutation or selection in evolution taken as a whole, and that should (though it hardly will) put an end to the endless debate over the internal and external direction of evolutionary trends. These apparent alternatives are lacking in reality; put in these terms they carry no weight: in truth, they are meaningless.

In opposition to the Darwinian tradition, "idealist morphology" has little trouble in showing that relations of descent are far from being the only ones to deserve consideration. Speculation upon the genetic series even raises questions in the philosophy of history (essential and accidental relations—the primitive and the simple—problem of stages) and cannot be treated as a summary of facts from zoological generation or descendence (Dacqué [3]). But "idealist morphology" restricts itself to vindicating its descriptive powers against the claims of mechanism. It situates the ideas which it introduces in *our* thought, and, in keeping with the Kantian tradition, reserves the interior of nature to an inaccessible reality. A truly statistical conception of evolution would, on the contrary, attempt to define vital being starting from phenomena; it would impose the prin-

2. G. G. Simpson, *The Major Features of Evolution* (New York: Columbia University Press, 1953), p. 59.

3. E. Dacqué, *Organische Morphologie und Pälaontologie* (Berlin: Borntraeger, 1935).—*Trans.*

ciples of an "evolutionary kinetic" free from any schema of timeless causality or constraint from microphenomena, and would openly admit a scalar structure of reality, a plurality of "space-time levels." Organisms and types would then appear as "traps for fluctuations," as "patterned jumbles," as variants of a sort of "phenomenal topology" (F. Meyer), without any break with chemical, thermodynamic and cybernetic causation.

Our purpose was to get to the appearance in nature of man and the human body. If the development of life is a "phenomenon," that is to say, if it is reconstructed by us on the basis of our own life, then it cannot be derived as an effect from a cause. Furthermore (and this is the difference between phenomenology and idealism), life is not a simple *object* for a *consciousness*. In previous courses we have shown that life and external nature are unthinkable without reference to perceived nature. Now we must think of the human body (and not "consciousness") as that which perceives nature which it also inhabits. Thus the relation between *Ineinander* which we thought we perceived can be recovered and confirmed. The object of the last part of the course was to describe the animation of the human body, not in terms of the descent into it of pure consciousness or reflection, but as a metamorphosis of life, and the body as the "body *of* the spirit" (Valéry).

The latter purpose would demand an "esthesiology," a study of the body as a perceiving animal. For there can be no question of analyzing the fact of birth as if a body-instrument had received from elsewhere a thought-pilot, or inversely as if an object called the body had mysteriously produced consciousness out of itself. We are not dealing here with two natures, one subordinate to the other, but with a double nature. The themes of the *Umwelt,* of the body schema, of perception as true mobility (*Sichbewegen*), popularized in psychology and nerve physiology, all express the idea of corporeality as an entity with two faces or two "sides." Thus the body proper is a sensible and it is the "sensing"; it can be seen and it can see itself; it can be touched and it can touch itself, and, in this latter respect, it comprises an aspect inaccessible to others, open in principle only to itself. The body proper embraces a philosophy of the flesh as the visibility of the invisible.

If I am capable of feeling by a sort of interlocking of the body proper and the sensible, I am capable also of seeing and recognizing other bodies and other men. The schema of the body proper, since I am able to see myself, can be shared by all other bodies, which I can also see. The body schema is a lexicon of corporeality in general, a system of equivalences between the inside and the outside which prescribes from one to the other its fulfillment in the other. The body which possesses senses is also a body which has desires and thus esthesiology expands into a theory of the libidinal body. The theoretical concepts of Freudianism are corrected and affirmed once they are understood, as suggested in the work of Melanie Klein, in terms of corporeality taken as itself the search of the external in the internal and of the internal in the external, that is, as a global and universal power of incorporation. The Freudian libido is not an entelechy of sex, nor is sex a unique and total cause but rather an ineluctable dimension outside of which nothing human can abide since nothing which is human is entirely incorporeal. A philosophy of the flesh finds itself in opposition to any interpretation of the unconscious in terms of "unconscious representations," a tribute paid by Freud to the psychology of his day. The unconscious is feeling itself, since feeling is not the intellectual possession of "what" is felt, but a dispossession of ourselves in favor of it, an opening toward that which we do not have to think in order that we may recognize it. Is the notion of an unconscious state adequate to the facts of repression, the mode of existence of the "primitive scene" and its power of seduction and fascination? The double formula of the unconscious ("I did not know" and "I have not always known it") corresponds to two aspects of the flesh, its poetic and its oneiric powers. When Freud presents the concept of repression in all its operational richness, it comprises a double movement of progress and regression, of openness toward the adult universe and of a relapse to the pregenital life, but henceforth called by its name, having become unconscious "homosexuality" (*From the History of an Infantile Neurosis*).[4] Thus the repressed unconsciousness would be a secondary formation, contemporary with the formation of a system of perception—consciousness—and the primordial unconsciousness would be a permissive being, the initial yes, the undividedness of feeling.

The preceding leads to the idea of the human body as a natural symbolism; an idea, rather than being final, announced, on the contrary, a sequel. We may ask what could be the relation between this tacit symbolism, or undividedness, and the artificial or conventional symbolism, which seems to be privileged, to open us toward ideal being and to truth. The relation between the explicit logos of the sensible world will form the topic of another series of courses.

4. *The Complete Works of Sigmund Freud,* vol. XVII (London: Hogarth Press, 1955).—*Trans.*